What people are saying about …

The Pursuit of

"This book is stern stuff: bracing, convicting, sobering. It calls us away from the shallowness and flimsiness of a Christianity glutted with novelties and agog at celebrities and calls us back to the wild, deep beauty—and terror—of God's sheer holiness. Ponsonby does more than describe holiness, though he does that brilliantly. He makes us ache, in every joint and marrow, for the Holy One and the holy life. Rise up, O church of God, and be done with lesser things."

Mark Buchanan, author of *Spiritual Rhythm: Being with Jesus Every Season of Your Soul*

"Warning: Don't read this book if you want to remain comfortable with your concept of holiness. Simon writes with precision, intellect, and passion on a subject mostly ignored in our own lives and in churches today. He grabs at the throat of passivity, calling for every Christian to get serious about a subject that's very serious to God. A must-read for those who long for God's holiness to be reflected in their lives and churches today."

Pat Harley, president of Big Dream Ministries

"This isn't a book that drives the worn-out Christian toward some standard of holiness through guilt and shame. This is a book that invites believers to the holiness that Jesus offers through grace and truth. Refreshingly honest, thoroughly biblical, and compellingly connected to church history."

Ed Underwood, pastor of Church of the Open Door and author of *When God Breaks Your Heart* and *Reborn to Be Wild*

THE PURSUIT OF THE HOLY

THE PURSUIT OF THE HOLY

A DIVINE INVITATION // SIMON PONSONBY

David C Cook®
transforming lives together

THE PURSUIT OF THE HOLY
Published by David C. Cook
4050 Lee Vance View
Colorado Springs, CO 80918 U.S.A.

David C. Cook Distribution Canada
55 Woodslee Avenue, Paris, Ontario, Canada N3L 3E5

David C. Cook U.K., Kingsway Communications
Eastbourne, East Sussex BN23 6NT, England

LCCN 2010928372
ISBN 978-0-7814-0366-5
eISBN 978-1-4347-0250-0

© 2010 Simon Ponsonby

The Team: Richard Herkes, Amy Kiechlin, Sarah Schultz, Caitlyn York, Karen Athen
Cover design: Studio Gearbox
Cover image: Veer Images, royalty-free

Printed in the United States of America
First Edition 2010

1 2 3 4 5 6 7 8 9 10

053110

To
Mark and Matt—
soldiers, preachers, friends;
there for me when I needed them.

Contents

Chapter 1
The Longing to Be Holy

May the God of peace make you holy all the way through. May your whole spirit, soul and body be kept blameless at the coming of the Lord Jesus Christ. (1 Thess. 5:23)[1]

We are about to take a journey. This will be no abstract theological study, nor a simple push for personal pietism, for that would be to set our sights too low. No, my longing is to see the church transformed so that we might transform society. I have written this book to offer pointers to the way and the what of that transformation.

In the late nineteenth century, there was a groundswell of longing for a deeper and more effective Christian life in the churches. In 1874, the Oxford Conference was organized by Canon Christopher, the famous rector of St Aldates, around the theme of "The Promotion of Scriptural Holiness," with an emphasis on the Spirit-filled life.

Fifteen hundred Christian leaders and theologians attended. The following year, another conference, the Keswick Convention, was held to teach further on the themes of the Spirit-filled life and sanctification. This became the great boiler house for evangelicalism in the twentieth century—influencing the Welsh Revival and Pentecostal beginnings in America as well as revivals in East Africa. Sparks that were fanned into a blaze began with a commitment to holiness. J. C. Ryle was caught up in this movement and produced his famous book *Holiness* in 1877.

Now, as we look to the future, we will also need to look into the past. Just as Isaac redug the wells of Abraham, which the Philistines had blocked up (Gen. 26:18), so we must explore wells of holiness that have been dug and then filled throughout the church's history. Here in the twenty-first century, it is time to open up those deep, old wells of holiness.

THE DARKNESS IS DEEPENING

"The darkness is deepening." So said Gandalf in Tolkien's classic The Lord of the Rings trilogy. And so it is for us. Faced with an unconvincing church, society is looking to alternatives.

Secularism has sold us a society without God, where material things are worshipped. We are also seeing the advance of fundamentalist *atheism* bent on the exorcism of theism. How can this be? Because the church has often lived as if God were dead. Yet concurrent with this, we are witnessing the rapid rise of a radical *Islam* that appeals to many who long for religious certainties and conviction, especially after finding in the church little more than a divided house or pious platitudes.

After years of greed on greed, the money markets have destabilized and banks themselves are bankrupt, while fat-cat bankers have retired early and buried their heads in their fat pay pensions. We have experienced an acute loss of confidence in the democratic political office, where spin has replaced conviction and pragmatism has eviscerated idealism. And we are seeing a moral meltdown, with prisons at breaking point, crime uncontrollable, families fatherless, morality a myth, and many of our streets filled with terror at feral gangs ready to knife to death innocents who do no more than look at them the wrong way.

And yet, while sinners are certainly responsible for their own sin, I don't entirely blame the world. They merely do what is in line with their natures: They sin. You cannot be surprised when sinners act sinfully—they have no power to purify themselves. Can a godless society be expected to be godly without seeing what godliness is? While the church may speak prophetically to the world about justice and righteousness, I don't think we can entirely blame the world for its unrighteousness. The church has all too often blended in with the world rather than revealed Christ and his ways to the world. We have failed to be that shining light, that salting influence. And so, as we fail to conform to Christ and the gospel we profess, the church has at times hindered, rather than helped, the world in coming to Christ. In fact, in some areas, the world appears to be ahead of the church, provoking her to action, especially in issues relating to social justice and the poor.

A HOLY PEOPLE CAN BE EXPECTED TO BE HOLY

So if the world is a mess, the church must shoulder some blame. Darkness cannot dispel itself. The demonic won't exorcise itself—Jesus said Satan cannot cast out Satan (Matt. 12:26). The darkness flees when a light is lit. But the church has often hidden the light by failing to preach the gospel or pietistically pursuing holiness by withdrawing from society. Sometimes she has even failed to have a light to lift by not truly believing the gospel. Somewhere along the line we have forgotten our vocation—to be "a chosen people, a royal priesthood, a holy nation" (1 Peter 2:9). Jesus said it is part of the church's role, through conforming to him and conveying him to the world, to be a sanctifying, salting influence in society (Matt. 5:13–16).

No one will listen to our gospel if we aren't living it. We cannot influence or infect society with something that has not yet infected us. A saltless salt cannot savor and flavor. The church cannot light a fire if she is not on fire. And so, faced with a society in crisis, in wickedness, it is time for judgment, repentance, *holiness* to begin in the family of God (1 Peter 4:17). We need a reformation, a revival—and holiness will be at the heart of it. The church must again find and follow Jesus—not as a doctrine to be believed but as a Lord to be served and a life to be lived. Only then can we speak with integrity and expect to be heard.

A holy church can influence an unholy world. Where Christ is seen, he is attractive, wooing and winning people to himself. I am not saying that everyone would turn to Christ if the church attained a great level of holiness, for the demonic and self-willed will always resist God. In fact, a holy church is more likely to be a persecuted church. But as the church lives for God, she will undoubtedly attract others to him. That is why C. S. Lewis could say,

> How little people know who think that holiness is dull.
> When one meets the real thing ... it is irresistible.[2]

And as Paul said, "Through us [God] spreads everywhere the fragrance of the knowledge of him" (2 Cor. 2:14).

HATING THE PSEUDO

Many years ago, when I arrived in the city of Oxford as a chaplain, I asked a graduate how I should best conduct myself. He replied, "Oxford hates the pseudo," implying that the university can spot a fake quickly. Well, my experience has since challenged that graduate's belief ... but one thing is for sure: The church cannot afford to be pseudo. There must be no pretense at piety because people can quite quickly distinguish the authentic from the imitation. They know a holy Christian when they see one, and they know a hollow one too. Old Testament theologian John Oswalt offered this stinging observation:

> The world looks on hateful, self-serving, undisciplined, greedy, impure people who nevertheless claim to be the people of God and says, "You lie."[3]

It is not as if we are addressing a marginal issue here—it is central. In the latest celebrated "revival" in the West, a feted evangelist suddenly walked off the stage and walked out on his wife. Claims of numerous extraordinary miracles could not be substantiated—not even one. I attended churches and watched ministers manipulate money out of church members for the promise of miracles. Pretense, fabrication, and nonsense were rife. Nothing new here, of course, but I groaned along with many others in the church: Where was the bride of Christ, making herself ready for Christ (Rev. 21:2)?

IS THAT SOMETHING IN YOUR EYE?

Recently I had my porch rebuilt and repainted. It was about a decade overdue, so I apologized to the painters and carpenters for the state it was in—including the mature cobwebs large enough to function as a windbreak. One of the builders replied, "No worries—I clean other people's gutters, but you should see the mess in my own house."

He is not the only one to neglect his own house, of course. The prophet Isaiah found himself in a similar position, metaphorically. Isaiah spoke more about holiness than any other prophet. It was part of his ministry to call the nations to holiness. Assuming the chapters of his book are in chronological order, it would appear that, although he was already established in his ministry of exposing wickedness and preaching warning and rebuke to God's people (chapters 1—5), he subsequently had a vision of God in the temple (chapter 6) that left him completely undone. In his vision, he saw angels crying, "Holy, holy, holy." As he stood before God, he knew it was not the nation of Judah that he must first target but himself, Isaiah the prophet: "Woe is me! For I am lost; for I am a man of unclean lips, and I dwell in the midst of a people of unclean lips" (Isa. 6:5 ESV). The prophet had preached the nations' guilt only to see his own.

When we see God, we see the superlative of holy. When we see the Holy One, we see ourselves as we are—sinful. We ought not preach against the sinfulness of society if we aren't also preaching against the sinfulness of the church. And lest we be hypocrites, we ought not do that before we have applied the message to the sinfulness of our own hearts (Matt. 7:1–5).

And so in this book, I want to broadcast an encouragement to gain a vision of God in his holiness *and* to see ourselves truly as we are. But of course we won't stop there. We must go on to know, as Isaiah knew, a deep cleansing from God's fire and a commissioning for his service. I do not believe that Isaiah had been a hypocrite—he had said what he saw in the world and what he heard from God; but lest he fall, thinking he stood tall, God also showed him himself. Now his message could be tempered by self-awareness, a much-needed humility in the face of burning-coal grace for the sinner.

I have often found that the most difficult aspect of being a minister is feeling a hypocrite. Many of us are ordained and given the title *Reverend*—we are to be revered as those set apart by God to minister on his behalf, to teach and lead people to him, and in prayer to represent him to the people and the people before him. What a privilege! What a burden! The fact is that we fail consistently to live up to the standard that we preach, teach, and exhort in others. Like Paul, sometimes "I do not do what I want, but I do the very thing I hate" (Rom. 7:15 ESV). This made Paul feel wretched, and I know that feeling—although sometimes, I confess, I resign myself to the presence of sin and weakness rather than feeling wretched or wrestling against it.

COMING TO TERMS WITH HOLINESS

It is instructive to think for a moment about the various terms in the English language surrounding holiness. Our word *holy* derives from the Old English *halig*, which itself came from the German *heilig*, referring to "health, happiness, wholeness."[4] The English language also employs words from the Latin *sanctus* (holy) in words like *saint, saintly*, and *sanctification*.

In the Old Testament, words based on *qds,* the Hebrew word for holy, appear over 850 times.[5] Holiness, then, is one of the most central concepts in biblical theology. The semantic origins of holiness relate to the word *cut* and have to do with distinction—standing out or being apart. It is preeminently the nature of God's own being and is then a derived characteristic of people and things as they exist in right relation to God. In the Old Testament, the word is applied to priests and their clothing, Israelites, Nazirites, Levites, firstborn human beings, prophets, offerings, the sanctuary and its furniture, inherited land and property, dedicated money and precious objects, the avoidance of certain mixtures (there were to be no garments made of both linen and wool, no crossbreeding of animals, no plowing with both an ox and an ass), the law, oil for anointing, incense in the sanctuary, water flowing from the temple or in a laver, places where God revealed himself, the land of Israel, Jerusalem, heaven, the Sabbath and feasts, Jubilee, covenant, and even, on occasion, war.

In the New Testament, *hagios,* which is Greek for "holy" or "saint," occurs over 150 times together with its associated words. *Hagios* means to be separate, dedicated, or consecrated to God. Originally, it was a religious concept of "the quality possessed by things and persons that could approach a divinity," that which was reserved for God and his service. It contained the sense of "perfect, pure and worthy of God."[6] The New Testament follows the Old in applying the word first to God and secondly to things and people. The first sense is located in terms of God; his Spirit; and his Son, Jesus, the Holy One of God. The second describes the people of God, the "saints" who are "holy ones."

God is holy. Holiness is his nature and character. It is not an attribute; it is who he is. He is the one who exists in holiness—perfection, beauty, purity, otherness. People and things are said to be holy by their relation to God, as they are offered by him or to him or before him. Days of rest, days of feasting, prophets and priests, gifts to God or from him, covenants and scriptures, angels and servants, temples and land, covenants and commandments, hands lifted in worship, lips offered in kisses to the brethren, the marriage bed, and mountains of revelation—all these can be holy by association with him. Holiness is infused into things or people that come close to God or exist for him.

One useful way to approach the meaning of holiness is to see how other words are placed in relation to it, often interpreting or applying it. In Scripture, the idea of holiness is found alongside cleanliness (Isa. 35:8); purity (1 Thess. 4:7); blamelessness (1 Thess. 3:13); glory (Ezek. 28:22); righteousness (Eph. 4:24); godliness (2 Peter 3:11); honor (1 Thess. 4:4); goodness (Ps. 65:4); truthfulness (Ps. 89:35); trustworthiness (Ps. 93:5); and awe (Ps. 111:9).[7] All of these help us understand what holy is and looks like. Holiness is a way of behaving that is determined by the being of God. David Peterson calls it a life "possessed by God"—a life that becomes like the God who possesses holiness.[8]

WHAT DO OTHERS MAKE OF THE HOLY?

The famous anthropologist Émile Durkheim made the startling claim that you don't need to have a notion of "god" to have a notion of holiness. He suggested holiness is more about social cohesion than religious devotion. From his observations of pagan tribes, he maintained that religion is not about a deity but the distinction between the "profane" and the "sacred"—a distinction expressed in a system of beliefs and practices that make certain objects and acts sacred, while others become mundane or profane. In a similar vein, Nobel Prize–winning Swedish archbishop Nathan Söderblom asserted that "holiness is the great word in religion—it is even more essential than the notion of God," and like Durkheim, he believed religion was all about this distinction between the sacred and the profane.[9]

What might this non-divine notion of holiness look like? Think about a game of soccer. There is no mention of a God, but it clearly exhibits all the signs of liturgy and sacrament for those who attend a holy event. The people gather together at their cathedral (the stadium) and, wearing their Sunday best (team colors, scarves and shirts), already feel involved in something bigger than the sum of its parts. They sit together and sing their worship (soccer chants). Then comes the moment of awe as the religious drama begins: The priests (players) gather on the Holy of Holies (field), and the liturgy of sacrifice begins at the referee's whistle. The offering (ball) is maneuvered to the altar (net) with the anticipation of a sacrifice (goal), at which the religious ecstasy of the crowd explodes in cheers. And the opposing team and their fans would presumably be the profane. Clearly, for many who attend, the match follows a very religious structure between sacred and profane, and for those involved, it has the sense of being a holy time without any sense of the divine!

What are believers to make of this? Rather than agree that a soccer game is a sense of the holy without a need for the divine, I would suggest we are looking here at a search for the divine and the holy that has gone astray and been misplaced in the secular. While a view of a soccer game as a spiritual event may be a helpful insight into how societies structure themselves in what may be seen as religious acts, this view really doesn't get to the heart of biblical holiness. Holiness is more likely to generate unease or even fear in people, as Rudolf Otto famously explored in his 1923 book, *The Idea of the Holy*.

HOLIER THAN THOU

It isn't only the notion of the holy that makes people uneasy. Holy people do too. Holy living is countercultural. When we go beyond private piety, we adopt an alternative lifestyle that becomes a public, political, and prophetic challenge. Nevertheless, some will always rise to the challenge and be attracted to authentic holiness.

So why do we not see more people attracted to the holy? Surely many reject the notion of holiness because they can't see any evidence of it in those who talk most about it—the church! In his major study on holiness, Stephen Barton said that

> the language and practices of holiness have atrophied
> under the impact of modernity and secularisation.[10]

Certainly we live in an age when many have rejected God and have no interest in imitating his holy character or obeying his commands to be holy. Barton also suggests that some who might be interested in holiness are put off by fear of receiving the snub "holier than thou."

As if hypocrisy or a holier-than-thou attitude in the church aren't bad enough, I think we do even more harm when we lay down the law but fail to offer any clues about how to actually be holy—when we point the finger but don't lift a finger to help people be holy. Gene Edwards wrote about the burdens placed on people in the name of holiness:

> Dear reader, virtually all of this counsel, all of those books, and every one of those sermons, is setting you up for failure, for guilt, and for a lifetime of frustration.[11]

He believes church has failed to show and offer the world the way to be conformed to holiness. That way is made possible only by Christ living in me and I in him (John 15:4), as I follow him not in a bubble of personal piety but as a member of the church, where we support and encourage each other toward that goal.

HOLINESS IS HAPPINESS AND WHOLENESS

We have already noted that the word *holiness* is related to the idea of wholeness. Holiness is not a negative word but supremely positive. It is a concept that points to perfection. To be holy is to be like God, in whom there is no imperfection, no blemish, not the slightest attribute or action that is anything less than the best.

If holiness is a primary reflection of the being of God, then our call and invitation to be holy is a call to be with God and like God. Sinfulness, though universal, is not natural to humankind—it entered with the fall of our first parents, Adam and Eve. Ever since then, we have acted just like them: We have sinned and rejected God's way and been expelled from God's presence. But God's longing for us to be holy, his longing to make us holy, is driven by his longing to restore us into his likeness, to bring us into his presence. Stephen Barton rightly said,

> To attend to holiness … is to attend to a matter that lies at the very heart of what it means to be and become fully human.[12]

So holiness is about becoming more human, as we are restored into the image of God. Holiness is becoming like God—Peter spoke of being "partakers of the divine nature" (2 Peter 1:4 ESV).

God the Holy One is the source of life; sinfulness separates us from holiness and so separates us from life. Holiness is a return to Eden's ideal and a taste of paradise. The holy life is a foretaste of heaven on earth. It is not God's burden for us but God's best for us.

H. L. Mencken scorned the pious attitude of the Puritan who feared that "someone somewhere may be enjoying themselves."[13] But those who fit that so-called Puritan depiction know nothing of true holiness. Here's an indicator to shatter one's theological categories: The Bible tells us that the marriage bed needs to be kept holy (Heb. 13:4). Though not his main point, the writer of Hebrews shows that the marriage bed (sexual union between husband and wife) is itself holy and pure. Sex between husband and wife is holy! Somehow sex points beyond itself to the eternal, self-giving, reciprocal relations within the Godhead, where the desire of the other is served rather than the self gratified. So all that joy, pleasure, excitement, fun, release, wholeness, and fulfillment in sex between marriage partners is a holy thing. Once we acknowledge that even something so joyful and releasing as sex, within God's ordained parameters, is holy, then we rightly challenge those assumptions that holiness is a stern and sour concept. Medieval spirituality spoke of the "three ways" in the spiritual journey: purgation, illumination, and union. Purifying and pursuing holiness through the Christian disciplines bring illumination, a revelation of God and ourselves that leads to more disciplines and a further response. But always the goal of the path to holiness is deeper union—intimate, personal, passionate languishing in love with God. The psalmist said that in God's presence there is fullness of joy, or as Anne Lamott put it, "Laughter is carbonated holiness."[14]

Any form of holiness that leads to someone looking like they just drank a gallon of vinegar is not biblical holiness; it is more likely Pharisaism. The church has lost something of this notion of holiness as happiness. We need to look at the Jews celebrating Sabbath, their holiest of times. Men gather in the streets, linking arms and dancing. Home is turned into a place of wonder, mystery, and glory as families welcome the Sabbath. How much more should the church now celebrate holiness joyfully, knowing that the Messiah Jesus has come and, in one day, by his death for us at Golgotha, taken away all our sin?

Sadly, delighting in holiness is not often the hallmark of modern Christianity. Jesus himself said that he wanted our joy to be complete and that this completion would come through "abiding in love." Abiding in love would come through obedience to his commandments (John 15:9–11 ESV). Clearly, then, we are presented with a divine set of equations that connects holiness with joy:

obedience = abiding in love = joy

disobedience = dislocation = dissatisfaction

All this we shall explore in the pages that follow.

LONGING TO BE CLEAN

There is hope. Despite all the church's failure to model holiness ... despite her all too often pointing judgmental fingers or laying heavy guilt trips on the world ... despite her own tendency to a holier-than-thou attitude, there is in society a wide awareness of sinfulness and a desire for holiness. Many long to be other than they are. The religious impulse can itself be a longing that is responding to the promptings of a holy God.

We all know what it is to feel dirty on the inside, and anyone can be made to feel dirty. The most unholy of places, the most God-forsaken, defiled, and profane, was that hell on earth at Auschwitz. There the demonized Nazis made every attempt to "desanitize" and dehumanize the Jews. The women had one tap for fourteen thousand worker inmates, and they were forbidden to wash. Their faces, caked in mud, baked by the sun, became covered in sores and scabs, crawling with lice and fleas. This treatment made it easier to regard the Jews as vermin and kill them as such. The Nazis worked hard to completely obliterate every trace of dignity and purity—turning the religious men's prayer shawls into women's underpants so that what once symbolized purity and devotion to God would be defiled by bodily discharges.

The traditional places for the Jewish woman to articulate holiness were in her home and in her diet, making a distinction between the sacred and the profane, offering her life and work as worship to God. But how could she be holy? How could she resist the literal and moral filth of Auschwitz? How could she still offer something to God? The women held on to the Jewish notion that the face is a powerful illustration of God turning to his people and the people turning to God. The face was a symbol of that sacramental communion. And so, though it was strictly forbidden, they would find precious water, even soap, and wash one another's faces. They would wash the faces of those going to the gas chambers, or even of those who had already been murdered.[15]

This was an act of protest against immorality and evil; it was a *no* to the profane and impure. It was a small but massive act of saying to God in this apparent hellhole that *we are for you, we want you, we want to be holy, the darkness will not cover us. Even here, we are for you, and we make space for you. Even in this filth, we choose to be holy, we need to be holy, we will be holy. Here, in this insane, inhuman, dehumanizing cesspit, we bear the image of God. Let our faces shine for you; and yours, O God, on us.*

YOU CLOTHE ME

I was struck recently by a little incident told to me by a retired prison chaplain. She explained that when entering the prison, everyone had to take off their coats and bags, be searched, and pass through airport-style scanners so that they could be checked for any drugs and other illicit things that might be smuggled to the prisoners. One day, after passing through, she got to her room and realized she had left her coat back at the check-in. She walked back only to find the guards all trying on her coat. When they saw her, they took it off and handed it back to her, looking very embarrassed. One of them apologized, explaining, "We were just seeing what it would be like to be holy."

He wasn't joking. They had recognized and accepted that this dear priest was a holy person. They knew she was very different—not just from the prisoners, but from themselves. And somehow, her clothing connected in their minds to the holiness they saw in her. They really did want to see what that holiness might feel like, and so they put on the holy chaplain's holy jacket just in case something holy might be transmitted to them!

When a British bishop is invited to stay with the Queen, he receives a formal letter stating what clothes he must bring and wear on what occasion: first, a sports jacket and corduroys for an informal country stroll; second, a clerical outfit for more formal meetings; and third, a dinner jacket for evening supper. You have to dress right for the Queen of England!

Holiness is about having the right clothing to be with the King of Kings (Matt. 22:11–12).

Of course, whatever our best efforts, we probably won't get it right! But we need not fear: The prophet Zechariah tells us about the time God invited Joshua the high priest, the most revered religious person in the nation of Israel, to stay (Zech. 3). The high priest was recognized by the fact that he wore the holiest of garments, designed just for his solo holy office (Ex. 28). He was regarded as the holiest of men in Israel, the one who offered sacrifices for the sins of the whole nation to God—the only one in Israel who could enter the Holy of Holies and look upon God's glory, on just one day of the year. The high priest was the icon of holiness to this holy people, yet Zechariah tells us that the Devil stood at his side accusing him of his sin and guilt.

Well, whatever the Devil's accusations were, they were immediately silenced by God's rebuke. Even so, the angel, seeing the stained clothes of the high priest, commanded them to be removed. Now, no Israelite could possibly conceive that this holy man, who wore the finest vestments symbolizing his holy office, could dress unworthily. But God sees right through us. The good news, however, is in what happened next. At God's command, the angel removed the filthy clothes from the high priest and declared, "See, I have taken away your sin, and I will put rich garments on you" (Zech. 3:4). And they placed new clean clothes on him and a new turban on his head.

If the holy high priest's garments were filthy in God's sight, what hope is there for us? Every hope! The Devil can find some sin and stain to accuse the best of us—but the good news is that God does not wish to accuse, condemn, or embarrass us. He wants to rebuke the accuser, he wants to remove our uncleanness, he wants to dress us in divine clothes so that we are fit to stand in his presence.

In the chapters that follow, we shall explore holiness in its many facets—its foundation, its absence, its beckoning, its counterfeit, its provision, its perfection, its practicalities, and its potential for the future of our world. Let the journey begin.

Chapter 2
The Holiness of God

The famous Cambridge Edwardian preacher P. T. Forsyth once claimed that "everything begins and ends in our Christian theology with the holiness of God."[1] I agree. The biblical story of God and man begins in Eden in Genesis 3 with holiness violated and ends in Revelation 21 in the Holy City with holiness restored. The giving of land, covenant, law, sacrifice, prophets, Redeemer, and Holy Spirit is all about establishing encounters between a holy God and an unholy people. Take the notion of holiness out of Christianity, and you have nothing much left to say, be, or do. Not for nothing did Jesus instruct his disciples that the first prayer, the first concern of his praying people, was "hallowed be your name" (Matt. 6:9 ESV)—treating as holy the name of a holy God.

But for many, holiness is not the first and last thing to be said of God. There are often two reactions if you mention the holiness of God—*indifference* or *anxiety*. God's holiness is not a popular theme in many churches. I have never attended a conference on the theme, seldom heard a sermon preached on it, all too rarely sung contemporary worship songs on holiness. This uneasy avoidance of the theme is nothing new—P. T. Forsyth picked up on the reticence by many to engage with the theme:

> I have sometimes thought when preaching that I saw a perceptible change come over my audience when I turned from speaking about the love of God to speak about the holiness of God. There was a certain indescribable relaxing of interest.[2]

I am concerned that in an attempt to connect with the world, many new forms of church are losing connection with God. Consumerist in their religious appetite, they want only the doctrines that don't disturb. While rightly trying to find fresh expressions of the faith in new culture, while wanting to be free from the oppression of legalistic religion, let us not throw the baby out with the bathwater. What is needed is not a rejection of the concept of holiness but a true appropriation of it.

Indifference to holiness may well be a self-protecting mechanism to the other common reaction at the opposite end of the spectrum: anxiety or fear. When many people hear the term, they have an awakening deep within of feelings of guilt or shame, like someone who panics for no apparent reason when they see a policeman. I received a remarkable letter from a lady brought up in a strict Brethren context, taught from a very young age that God was terrifying. She wrote that when she was a girl,

> I used to wake up shaking in bed when a jumbo took off from the nearby airport, as I thought it was the second coming and I was in for it…. I often struggled to read the Bible as all I seemed to find was punishment and condemnation…. I saw life as a race-horse sees the track, narrow and something to be got out of the way as quickly as possible, involving the maximum amount of suffering so our eternal rest at the end could be reached when "life in all its fullness" was to begin…. God was angry, never satisfied, anti-women, demanding, a God who was gracious but I had to work so hard to be in that place before he would bestow his grace on me.[3]

The good news is that she eventually broke through this false understanding of God: "I realized that I had been worshipping a false god."

Both these reactions—a yawning indifference or a terrifying paralysis—demonstrate a complete failure to understand the nature of God in his holiness. It is vital for a healthy church and an effective witness that we understand aright the core of God's revelation as the Holy One. I fear that many are quick to make God in their image rather than understand we are made in his. Indeed, the philosopher Feuerbach criticized Christians over a century ago for making a God that was just man writ large, while the father of psychoanalysis, Freud, said our notion of God is often just the projection of our repressed infant longing for a father onto a heavenly figure. Such criticisms are not always so far from the truth, as many people's visions of God owe little to Scripture and much to their psychology. At worst, our imaginary conception of God is little more than an idol with a few proof texts to clothe it.

HOLINESS IS NOT A HOBBY FOR GOD

I believe that the doctrine of the holiness of God, rightly understood, is among the most exhilarating and motivating of all doctrines we could speak about, for to address this subject is to get at the very core of who God is. The Puritan Thomas Brooks said, "God's holiness is his nature, God's nature is his holiness." Holiness in humans or things or angels is a quality, something derived and dependent—but in God, it is his very being. James Muilenburg understood holiness not as the preeminent attribute of God but as the "innermost reality to which all others are related."[4]

At this point, some might counter that love is the innermost reality defining God's being. Since Augustine, love has been treated as God's primary attribute, defining the intertrinitarian relations and relationship with creation. While not diminishing that all God is and all God does is loving, nevertheless at his throne the seraphim do not declare the thrice-loving God but the thrice-holy God. His holiness is loving, and his love is holy; the two are indivisible, but I am inclined to consider holiness as the core of God's being. A. W. Tozer said,

> Holiness is the way God is. To be holy he does not conform to a standard. He is that standard. He is absolutely holy with an infinite incomprehensible fullness of purity.[5]

Holiness is intrinsic to God's name and his nature. As Jerry Bridges said, holiness is "as necessary as his existence."[6] All God says and does is holy; holiness is the perfection of all his attributes. If you like technical terms, Professor John Webster said that God's holiness is ontological (core to his being)—not an attribute but the perfection of all his attributes.[7] All God does in his action is holy because God is in himself the Holy One.

> God is holy, and therefore holiness characterizes all
> God's ways; in all that he does he is holy, and can no
> more not be holy than he can not be God.[8]

God swears by his holiness (Amos 4:2) and swears by himself (Amos 6:8)—suggesting the two are interchangeable. God is called "the Holy One"—a proper name (Job 6:10; Isa. 40:25; 43:15; Ezek. 39:7; Hos. 11:9; Hab. 1:12; 3:3)—and also "the Holy One of Israel" (2 Kings 19:22; Isa. 1:4; 43:3; Jer. 50:29).

Holiness may be defined as "the majesty and moral purity of God"[9]; it expresses God's being as "wholly other"—transcendent, unapproachable, distinctly other to creatureliness: "I am God and not man, the Holy One among you" (Hos. 11:9). William Greathouse said that the axiom of holiness is that God is God, creature is creature.[10] Kierkegaard called it the "infinite qualitative distinction." God alone is holy in himself; creatures or created things derive all holiness from the Holy One. Holiness comes through access to divinity.

God's holiness is breathtaking. The psalmist praised the "splendor of his holiness"—what the old King James version famously translated as "the beauty of holiness" (Ps. 29:2; 96:9). The Hebrew text

can be taken either way—we are praising God's holiness, or we ourselves are holy as we worship him. Either way, a holy people praise a
holy God. But we should probably take it to refer to God's holiness
(1 Chron. 16:29). Gerald McDermott rightly spoke of "loving God
for the beauty and sweetness of his moral greatness."[11]

God's holiness is exclusive. Without holiness, no one may see the
Lord (Heb. 12:14)—it was God's holiness and human sinfulness that
separated Adam and Eve from Eden.

God's holiness is embracing. God is the high and lofty one who
inhabits eternity yet dwells with those who are contrite and lowly in
spirit (Isa. 57:15).

God's holiness is gracious. Karl Barth's detailed treatment of God's
holiness is titled "The Grace and Holiness of God."[12] Holiness and
grace go hand in hand, always turning to humanity in love, seeking
to forgive, heal, redeem, restore. Grace follows holiness.

God's holiness is humble. There is a "unity of his transcendence
and condescendence"[13] by which the Holy One embraces us in grace.
There is nothing haughty in God's holiness. It is holiness that stoops
low.

God's holiness is relational. The covenant and the land and the law
and the sacrifices are given to facilitate and maintain the presence of
a holy God dwelling with his chosen people, Israel.

SEEING THE HOLY ONE

The ancients believed that to see God was to die (Gen. 32:30; Judg.
13:22), for no one without holiness could see the Lord and live (Heb.
12:14); his blazing holiness would burn up all without a pure heart,
and no one is that pure. And so it was that only the Son could truly

gaze on his Father and see as he is seen (John 1:18). Nevertheless many others had visions of God, seeing him hidden in cloud, on a mountain, in fire, above the ark of the covenant, glimpsing him from their hiding. The very name *Israel,* which generally is taken to mean "he struggles with God" (following Jacob's wrestling at night with an angel of the Lord in Genesis 32), is also understood to mean "one who sees God." And the great first-century father of Jewish thought, Philo, as well as the Greek church fathers, understood in this way. Israel had seen God—and survived!

It is often said that holiness is a prerequisite for any encounter with God. Indeed, Jesus said, "Blessed are the pure in heart, for they will see God" (Matt. 5:8), and this idea is a mainstay of much holiness spirituality. However, the crucial texts in Exodus 3 and Isaiah 6, where Moses and Isaiah saw God, were encounters not based on individual holiness but rather revealing God's holiness and human sinfulness. Let's take a close look at these two encounters.

TAKE OFF YOUR SHOES (EXODUS 3)

In this narrative, Moses—former crown prince of Egypt, now a runaway shepherd—is leading a flock of sheep in the desert when he receives a revelation from God and a commission to lead God's own flock, Israel, through the desert.

The angel of the LORD appeared to him ... (Ex. 3:2)

The first thing that stands out is that the divine visit is a divine initiative. This is an event all of the Holy One's making. Moses is not in prayer, in a temple, in an act of devotion or consecration, acting out his religion. He is not looking for the Holy One, not expecting the Holy One to come. The initiative is God's; it is free and sovereign and not based on response or requirement. Holiness can draw near to us even when we are not drawing near to the holy. This initiation is a great condescension, for the Lord, the God of the universe who created all things and sustains all things by his powerful word, comes and speaks. The holy made lowly in a bush! No great vision of a mountain-sized diamond—just a mundane desert plant.

…in flames of fire from within a bush. (v. 2)

Fire indicates purging, cleansing, refining—it is necessary for life, but come too close and you risk death. Mysterious, glorious, fascinating, and frightening, the Holy One is an all-consuming fire. God appears but remains hidden. His concealment is grace, for were God to fully manifest himself, Moses would surely die. The Holy One is present as fire in the bush, yet the bush survives—God is present to Moses, and Moses, too, will survive. That is the grace of the holy.

Moses saw that though the bush was on fire it did not burn up. So Moses thought, "I will go over and see this strange sight.…" (vv. 2–3)

Moses had doubtless seen many bushes on fire when the desert heat caused spontaneous fires in the dry twigs. But this is different—flames and yet the bush remains? And so he goes to take a look, out of interest, little knowing what God has in store. The Holy One gets Moses' attention, ready to work a revolution.

God called to him from within the bush, "Moses!
Moses!" And Moses said, "Here I am." (v. 4)

There is no indication this voice is overwhelming; Moses does not run. It is a voice that welcomes a response, a dialogue. The Holy One communicates with us. The Holy One knows—he knows where to find us (in the desert); he knows our name (Moses); he knows the plans he has for us ("I am sending you to Pharaoh"); he knows our family details ("your brother Aaron is coming"). He knows us, and he wants us to know him. This revelation of himself establishes a relationship with Moses. Moses replies, "Here I am"—he does not seek to dismiss the voice as the effect of sunstroke, nor ignore the voice, nor hide from it. He is willing to engage and respond. How many times has the Holy One spoken to us, and yet we crowd his voice out of our minds?

"Do not come any closer," God said. "Take off your
sandals, for the place where you are standing is holy
ground.... I am the God of your father, the God of
Abraham, the God of Isaac and the God of Jacob."
(vv. 5–6)

God reveals himself as the Holy One. The ground is now holy by virtue of God's appearance, and Moses must keep a respectful distance. Scrub desert bush becomes sanctuary because God stands there, infusing it with purity. God welcomes Moses nearer, but there is a point that Moses may not pass for his own safety! Moses must not move too close lest he be consumed. We might ask, How can something like a bush sustain the pure presence of God and not be consumed, while Moses will be destroyed if he comes too near?[14] Perhaps the answer lies in the fact that the rest of creation, unlike humankind, is not made in God's image; it is not sentient, not spiritual, not eternal, not moral, not confronted with divine revelation and divine decree. Consequently, unlike humanity, it cannot be morally judged or condemned—God's moral fire cannot break out against it. An amoral—and thus guiltless—bush won't be consumed by God's immanent presence, whereas a sinful and guilty Moses in close proximity to God would precipitate a moral eruption on God's part. God can remain within the bush that burns but is not consumed, whereas Moses must keep his distance.

God asks Moses to remove his sandals, possibly because of the filth they have stood in or as a prophetic gesture of respect. In the East, shoes were—and still are—removed as a sign of humility before one who is greater. Slaves always went barefoot. The intimacy and invitation do not remove the distinction. Moses must not be irreverent. One day, many years after Moses' encounter with God, the Holy One in flesh will wash filthy feet and have his own feet defiled by nails so that he may wash us more deeply. But for now, this act fulfills righteousness.

At this, Moses hid his face, because he was afraid to look at God. (v. 6)

Moses is intrigued by the bush fire and surprised by the voice that knows his name, and he feels able to come close and to speak in response. The presence of the Holy One has not intimidated him into a quivering mute. But once the Holy One behind the voice is named, shock and awe take over. Moses has been in the presence of Pharaoh before, but now he is in the presence of God. He doesn't merely turn away but hides his face (perhaps in his hands) because he wants neither to see God nor God to see him. He is suddenly all too aware of his creatureliness and sinfulness.

What follows is a dialogue in which Moses will receive a commission to go and lead God's beloved people, whose cries have come up to him, out of slavery in Egypt. God has not forgotten and will not forsake his promise to Abraham, Isaac, and Jacob. It is time for that promise to be fulfilled.

So what can we learn from this text about the Holy One?

- God's holiness doesn't preclude his *visitation* to sinners—he came to Moses.
- God's holiness doesn't preclude his *invitation* to sinners—he welcomed Moses to come to him.
- God's holiness doesn't preclude his *revelation* to sinners—he disclosed himself to Moses.
- God's holiness doesn't preclude his *condescension* toward sinners—he spoke from a mere bush.
- God's holiness doesn't preclude his *communication* with sinners—he dialogued with Moses.
- God's holiness doesn't preclude his *compassion* for sinners—he cares for the suffering of his people.
- God's holiness doesn't preclude his *commission* of sinners—he sent Moses to deliver them.

WOW OR WOE? (ISAIAH 6)

No doubt if you asked many people whether they would like an encounter with God, they would say, "Sure, why not?" At its peak, this longing for encounter is the mark of mystic and charismatic spirituality. But the experience of Moses, and certainly the experience of Isaiah that we now turn to, should cause us to be cautious. In fact, you can read of stories from the Azusa Street revival when the sense of God's glory was so immanent that the preacher hid inside the pulpit!

Today many Christians have lost a sense of awe in the presence of God and replaced it with a nonchalant, even flippant irreverence. Is it because they have a narrow grasp of his revelation in Scripture and little desire for personal experience of him beyond a subjective sentimental notion of God as love? J. Sidlow Baxter rightly noted:

> The revelation of the love of God must be safe-guarded by due recognition of His awful power and holiness.... One of the faults of certain modern theology is the mental divorcing of the Divine love from the Divine power and holiness.[15]

> *In the year that King Uzziah died, I saw the Lord ...*
> *(Isa. 6:1)*

Isaiah has a vision. We don't know whether it was mystical, in a dream or vision, or even a physical catching up to heaven (like Paul's in 2 Corinthians 12:1–4). As with Moses' encounter, God initiates this vision. Isaiah is passive—he does not go after God; the vision comes to him. We know the temple was in the vision, but we don't know whether the vision occurred when Isaiah was in the temple. However, we do know when it occurred: "In the year that King Uzziah died" sets the vision in the concrete reality of history. The king of Judah's death meant the nation was left unstable, susceptible, and vulnerable to Assyria's growing menace. So now Isaiah is given a vision that impresses an important fact: The king is dead—long live the King of Kings!

Uzziah is infamous for dishonoring the holiness of God by intending to offer incense in the temple sanctuary—something only a priest was allowed to do (2 Chron. 26:16–22). Uzziah, swollen with his own pride and achievement, had disrespected the holiness of God and, as a result, was struck down with leprosy. If Isaiah hadn't really gotten it before, he certainly now had impressed on him just how holy God is.

I saw the Lord seated on a throne, high and exalted,
and the train of his robe filled the temple. (v. 1)

The throne of Judah may have been vacant or unstable, but there is One who sits on the only throne that really matters, One who rules and reigns. "The Lord" is *adonai* in Hebrew—our sovereign master, none other than Yahweh, Lord, Almighty God, and King of all the universe. God's throne is not vacant. There is no power vacuum.[16]

This throne of the sovereign Lord of the universe is *high and exalted* over every other throne in Isaiah's world—Judah, Israel, Egypt, Babylon, Assyria—and exalted over every throne that would (and will) arise in history. Only God is high and lifted up. Those who set themselves up in pride, like Uzziah or arrogant Babylon (Isa. 14:4, 13) will be humbled.

I don't believe that Isaiah sees God's face, but rather that he sees just the hem of his garment flowing down the throne, filling the temple. That alone is sufficient to strike fear and terror into God's good prophet. Victorian prince of preachers C. H. Spurgeon once said, "There is nothing little about God!"

> *Above him were seraphs, each with six wings: With two wings they covered their faces, with two they covered their feet, and with two they were flying. (v. 2)*

These seraphim are ministering angels who herald the glory of God and give him glory day and night. Do not think in terms of round-faced baby cherubs with harps; these are awesome creatures whose name, *seraphim,* means "fiery" or "burning ones" and doubtless reflects their being. They are ablaze because they dwell in God's presence. Occasionally the term *seraph* refers to a snake or serpent (Num. 21:6; Isa. 14:29), and the link is not certain, but it may be telling us that these angelic seraphs have serpentine form—or perhaps the snake is named after the seraph because its sting is fiery.[17]

They have three pairs of wings—one pair that covers their faces, protecting them from gazing on God; one pair that covers their feet; and one pair by which they fly. The sense is of a need to cover up in the presence of a holy God. But they are not prostrate or paralyzed by fear; they are flying and worshipping and heralding God's glory—calling antiphonally to one another:

> *Holy, holy, holy is the LORD of hosts … (v. 3 ESV)*

They sing first and foremost of God's holiness—not his love or his power or any other attribute. Old Testament scholar Professor John Oswalt says the threefold repetition is the strongest form of all superlatives in Hebrew idiom.[18] The prophet Jeremiah repeated a phrase three times for emphasis and completeness (Jeremiah 7:4), and the notion of "three days" is a biblical motif for completeness. Traditional Jewish emphasis was generally to say something twice, as in "Truly, truly," or "Moses, Moses"; but the threefold repetition of a word is what Moberly called "super-superlative,"[19] and this form is found nowhere else in the Bible apart from John's vision of worship in heaven, which repeats the call "Holy, holy, holy" (Rev. 4:8). Declaring God to be both utterly complete and utterly unique in holiness is the defining vision of worship in heaven. Can we say that the theme of holiness features as strongly in our worship and praise as it evidently does in heaven?

> *...the whole earth is full of his glory. (v. 3)*

He is not just the God who is glorious in his temple or in Judah and Israel. He is no mere regional or national deity—God is the Lord of the whole earth, which both manifests his glory and exists to give him glory. God's majesty, authority, glory, divinity, and beauty extend universally. Yahweh is not the "God of the gaps"—not the *deus ex machina* gone walkabout. He is the King enthroned above the universe, filling it with his glory.

> *At the sound of their voices the doorposts and thresholds*
> *shook and the temple was filled with smoke. (v. 4)*

There is nothing muted, gentle, calm, or peaceful about this worship. It booms out, shaking the very foundations of the temple of God. Worship that "rocks," we might say. This worship affects all the senses—including the smell of the incense that is perhaps a shield of protection safeguarding all from the blazing glory of God, which, if seen directly, would be blinding like the sun at high noon. John Oswalt said, "The Holy God is not to be surveyed casually with unveiled eyes."[20] Surely that is why God, even when personally leading Israel through the wilderness, was hidden in cloud and fire.

> *"Woe to me!" I cried. "I am ruined!" (v. 5)*

Fools rush in where angels fear to tread. This vision elicits no wow, just woe. Many of our churches today are after the wow factor—the excitement, the thrill, the sensation. But a true encounter with God the Holy One leaves us broken, exposed, despairing, undone. This prophet had preached "woe" to others (5:8, 11, 18, 20, 21, 22) and now pronounces it upon himself. He believes himself "ruined"—the Hebrew word means "destroyed," and its form suggests he feels he is already destroyed. This is an almost annihilating experience from which he can never recover. Why does he feel this way? Because he is but a human, and God is God; because he is a mere creature, and God is Creator; and, mostly, because he is aware of his sinfulness before God's blazing holiness.

> *I am a man of unclean lips, and I dwell in the midst of*
> *a people of unclean lips; for my eyes have seen the King,*
> *the LORD of hosts! (v. 5 ESV)*

God doesn't tell Isaiah he is sinful—he doesn't need to. As light reveals darkness, God's holiness exposes man's sinfulness. The word Isaiah applies to himself, *unclean,* constitutes about the furthest condition removed from holiness. He is no different from the rest of his people he has preached to; he is a sinner. Why focus on lips? Because it is with their lips that the seraphim have praised God—yet how can Isaiah do the same when he is so sinful? He has spoken of God with those lips. Now that he sees his sin, he wonders how he ever dared! The speech on our lips is, in Jewish thought, the focus of the overflow of the heart (Matt. 12:34), and Isaiah's lips, revealing his heart and his very being, are defiled. He never saw it before, but then he had never seen God before. I wonder what part of you would feel exposed and sinful in his holy presence: mind, mouth, hands, heart, eyes?

> *Then one of the seraphs flew to me with a live coal in his hand, which he had taken with tongs from the altar. With it he touched my mouth and said, "See, this has touched your lips; your guilt is taken away and your sin atoned for." (vv. 6–7)*

Oh, what grace! Isaiah is not destroyed for looking on God while he is still unclean. Instead, he is cleansed. Isaiah doesn't ask for this, and he knows he doesn't deserve it. He certainly doesn't expect it—he expects to die. But God graciously, freely cleanses him. The fiery ones bring fire from the hot coals on the temple altar. The altar is the place of sacrifice—and the place of sacrifice is the place of cleansing. The coals are not to damage Isaiah's lips but to purify them, for "God does not reveal himself to destroy us, but rather to redeem us."[21]

General Booth once said, "Great as God is, there are some things he cannot do—he cannot pass over sin, he must deal with it in some way … but there are some things he can do—he can forgive sin as soon as it is confessed."

Then I heard the voice of the Lord saying, "Whom shall I send? And who will go for us?" And I said, "Here am I. Send me!" (v. 8)

God doesn't destroy Isaiah; he employs him. This vision is intended as a recommission. Just as God met Moses in a burning bush to send him as his ambassador, so God meets Isaiah to send him out as his prophet. God asks the question, "Who?" and Isaiah volunteers: "What about me? Here I am." He's unworthy but not unwilling. And God replies, "Go!"

The burden of Isaiah's message to the nation of Israel and to the other nations would now reflect his own experience—it would speak of not only the holiness of God but also the grace of God. Following this vision of his holy God and his sinful self, Isaiah would speak of "the holy" no less than a further fifty times in his prophecies, and his preferred title for God would be "the Holy One of Israel." That phrase occurs twenty-six times in Isaiah and only six in the rest of the entire Old Testament. John Oswalt said, "Whatever else this experience did for Isaiah, it convinced him that God alone is holy."[22] Isaiah never recovered from this encounter with the Holy One of Israel.

What may we learn from Isaiah's encounter with God?

- We can serve God for years, even as his prophet and priest, and not really know him.
- Whatever our social, personal, or political situation or crisis, God is on the throne, he is in power, and he is King.
- Worship like that of the angels is the great ministry of those who would be near God.
- God is the thrice-holy God—he is preeminent and perfect in holiness, and this is the first thing to be understood and said of him.
- Whoever we may think we are and whatever we may think we've done for God, it takes some form of encounter to give us a true perspective of ourselves.
- God's holiness won't destroy us if we repent of our sinfulness.
- God is gracious, forgiving, and cleansing, removing sin in an instant.
- God will employ us in his service, despite past failure, if we will only say, "Here I am."

> *The only hope, or else despair*
> *Lies in the choice of pyre or pyre.*[23]

ENCOUNTERING THE HOLY

Too often, our concept of God trivializes the profound. I fear many are quick to entertain images of God drawn from popular novels that present God in forms we can more comfortably identify with—God as familiar, tender, gentle, even maternal. But it is the God of Isaiah's vision with whom we must come face-to-face. It is the thrice-holy God who makes angels cover their faces, thresholds quake, and prophets moan "undone."

I once heard a preacher recall a sermon he preached on Isaiah's vision of God. He decided to make no appeals and give no application. He wanted the Word to bear its own weight and carry its own message to those present. With the best of his ability he presented the vision of God as seen by Isaiah … unaware of its effect. In his congregation was a family completely traumatized because that very week they had discovered that their daughters had been serially abused by a relative for three years. The girls had contracted sexually transmitted diseases and were now receiving medical care. The abuser was in custody; the parents were distraught.

Three months later the father came to the preacher and said, "Pastor, these have been the worst three months of our lives. You know what's gotten us through? The vision of God's holiness from your sermon [three months before on Isaiah 6]: It has been the only rock in our lives." Why? How? Because God's holiness makes us aware that we are all sinners; because God's holiness makes us aware that he is righteous and that justice will be done; because God's holiness is big enough to lift our eyes and hearts beyond our immediate pain and problems to a more perfect vision of reality. We know that, one day, God's holiness will put all things right.

Chapter 3
The Sinfulness of Us

A WALK IN THE DARK

On arriving at the coffee shop where I intended to write this chapter on sin, I pondered for a moment how many times I might have sinned during the five-hundred-yard walk from my church. The Spirit brought to mind my interest in an attractive woman, anger at the car that pulled out in front of a cyclist, subtle pride and indifference to a beggar, unbelief that God would help me today, annoyance that my usual seat in the coffee shop was taken, disdain for a man I saw who once verbally patronized me, and pride at being greeted and engaged in conversation by a world-famous theologian. And those were just the sins I was immediately aware of in five minutes and five hundred yards!

It's not easy to walk in the Spirit—perhaps I should have stayed in bed. Oh, how right John was when he said, "If we say we have no sin, we deceive ourselves, and the truth is not in us" (1 John 1:8 ESV)! Brainerd said on November 27, 1742, "Surely I may well love all my brethren; for none of them is so vile as I; whatever they do outwardly, yet it seems to me none is conscious of so much guilt before God. O my leanness, my barrenness, my carnality, and past bitterness, and lack of a gospel temper!"[1]

> Were it not for God's holiness, I would probably be unaware of such sins;
>
> were it not for God's holiness, I would probably not care about such sins;
>
> were it not for God's grace, I would be drowning in even more sin;
>
> were it not for God's grace, I'd have no hope of freedom from such sin;
>
> were it not for God's grace, I'd be in danger of judgment for such sins.

THE HOLINESS OF GOD EXPOSES THE SINFULNESS OF MAN

The closer we come to God, the clearer we see ourselves. His holiness exposes our sinfulness, his perfection our imperfection, his standard our failure, his purity our stain. Approaching God can be a crushing experience. Bishop J. C. Ryle said,

> I am persuaded the more light we have, the more we

> see our own sinfulness; the nearer we get to heaven,
> the more we are clothed with humility.[2]

We saw previously that Moses was welcomed into God's presence and told to take off his shoes (Ex. 3), for he stood on holy ground. He was warned not to come too close in case God's blazing holiness broke out and destroyed him. We saw how Isaiah, already God's prophet, had a vision of the Holy One (Isa. 6) and bewailed himself as undone, destroyed, a man of unclean lips. We considered Zechariah's revelation of the high priest, the godliest man in the land, who stood before God (Zech. 3) yet was clothed in filthy rags and gave grounds for Satan to accuse him.

Peter similarly, when he encountered Jesus Christ, the Holy One of God, displaying his power in a miraculous catch of fish, declared, "Go away from me, Lord; I am a sinful man!" (Luke 5:8). The godly centurion whose servant was sick sent a messenger to Jesus, appealing to him to have mercy and heal the servant by simply speaking a word because he regarded himself too sinful to have the Holy One in his home: "Don't trouble yourself, for I do not deserve to have you come under my roof. That is why I did not even consider myself worthy to come to you" (Luke 7:6–7).

To see God, to encounter Christ, is—among other things—to be immediately conscious of failing, falling far from God's perfection, beauty, glory, and purity. His light exposes all blemishes. C. S. Lewis, drawing from the Puritans, once wrote,

> One essential symptom of the regenerate life is a
> permanent, and permanently horrified perception

of one's natural and (it seems) unalterable corruption. The true Christian's nostril is to be continually
attentive to the inner cesspool.[3]

SO WHO'S TO BLAME?

If we are to understand the beauty of holiness, we are forced to face
the ugliness of sinfulness. To see God in his perfection is to confront
ourselves in our imperfection. The subject of sin, of course, makes
us wince. Karl Rahner, the famous German Catholic theologian,
notes that the word *sin* is generally avoided these days and suggests
that this is both a reaction to the moralistic and legalistic notion of
sin (people don't like being told they are sinners) and the result of
a loss of purity in our idea of God (people don't really believe in a
wholly holy God).[4] This loss of the themes of human sin and divine
holiness in modern society rather reflects the age-old avoidance
of Adam, who, in his guilt, shame, and fear, attempted to cover
up, hiding his naked sin with leaves and hiding himself from God
behind trees. The revelation of God's holiness, which exposes our
sinfulness, causes us either to run to God for mercy, confessing our
sins, or, more often, to deny our sins and even deny the existence
of a God as a basis for morality. As Dostoyevsky and Nietzsche
noted in their different ways, when there is no God, everything is
permissible.

We may lose the concept of sin (and God), but that doesn't mean
we necessarily lose the awareness of their reality—sin or evil must
simply be ascribed to something other than personal crime against a
personal divine.[5]

Buddhism, for instance, has no real concept of sin or a God who can be sinned against—rather, the universe is ordered on the basis of karma, in which all actions simply have consequences. Similarly, Hinduism views sin as an act against the moral order or ourselves. Good deeds can make up for past wrongdoing. Gnosticism blames sin on the human connection with matter. Salvation is achieved through separating ourselves from matter and moving into the spirit realm through secret knowledge and religious practices. Nurturists (Locke, Rousseau) will blame sin on the social and educational environment in which an individual develops. For all of these, overcoming sin is a matter of "enlightenment."

Psychotherapists like Freud and Jung may blame the individual's parents or emotional and psychological adjustment; here, overcoming sin is a matter of therapy—bringing transformed understanding. Darwinians will blame sin on the biological and possibly social development of the individual's race—overcoming sin requires time for further evolution. Marxists or communists will lay blame for sin at the door of oppressive bourgeoisie capitalist commercial and political systems for producing social ills, and here, overcoming sin is a matter of political revolution.[6]

In all such worldviews, sin or evil is rarely the individual's fault and is certainly not the transgressing of a divine moral order. Usually the problem lies in influences from outside—environmental, intellectual, or social factors. And so we don't need to hold any individual responsible for "sin"—in fact, we may prefer to see people more as victims.

How might we respond to these alternative ideas? We can ask whether any of them actually work in overcoming sin. Has Marxism led to less sin? The twenty to fifty million killed by Stalin suggests otherwise! Has Darwin's evolutionary development led to less sin? Humans are the cruelest of creation's creatures. The advance of history shows no clear advance in morality! Does education and transformation of social context reduce sin? It has been said that to educate a man in prison who stole an iron railway spike, without changing his heart, will lead only to his attempt to try and steal the whole railroad next time! An Old Etonian once told me there was an Old Etonian in every jail in the world. So much for the finest of education and privilege!

COMING TO TERMS WITH SIN

Our word *sin* comes from the Old English *syn* which, together with related words in Old Norse, High German, and Old French, is descended from the Latin root *sons,* meaning "guilty." Its Old English use pointed to the idea of an offense or wrongdoing, "an act which is regarded as a transgression of the divine law and an offense against God."[7]

In the Old Testament, the main Hebrew terms for sin all convey the sense of transgression or deviation from the right path, as dictated by covenant and law, resulting in guilt. Old Testament scholar W. Günther said, "Yahweh is the yardstick for right and wrong."[8] His covenants with his people and his commandments and law and word through his prophets express his normative will:

> Sin is a falling away from relationship of faithfulness with God and disobedience to his commands.[9]

Rahner said:

> Sin is above all revolt, offense, irritation and
> contempt, and has the character of a violation of
> the covenant, and indeed of adultery as regards
> Yahweh.[10]

God takes personally the violation of his law; sin is against him, even if the act is against our fellow humans or even the land. Thus sin, says Rahner, is the opposite of loving God and our neighbor.

In the Old Testament, talk of sin always has the individual act of transgression of the law in view, although the source of this transgression is recognized as originating from a corrupted heart that desperately needs renewing (Ps. 51:10; Jer. 32:39; Ezek. 11:19).[11] The New Testament expands the scope to a state of being, not simply actions we do or fail to do as we veer off course from God's covenant and law. Sin is seen as defilement of the whole of human nature. The Greek New Testament terms center around the word *hamartia*. Originally this referred to the idea of missing the mark, being mistaken, and so failing to share in something. The term was used in archery of an arrow falling short or failing to hit the target. It developed into a term conveying an offense against morals and laws both divine and human.[12] It occurs nearly three hundred times in the New Testament and becomes the "comprehensive expression of everything opposed to God."[13]

What motivates this rebellion, this transgression of law and command and covenant? Calvin spoke of it as a disregard for God. Augustine defined sin as pride—an egocentricity, a putting of one-self at the center. Kierkegaard spoke of sin as the opposite of faith, whereby we trust in the finite rather than the infinite. Karl Barth spoke of it as unbelief that leads to pride, disobedience, and apostasy. J. C. Ryle, in his classic treatment of holiness, said sin consists in

> doing, saying, thinking or imagining anything that is not in perfect conformity with the mind and law of God.... The slightest outward or inward departure from absolute mathematical parallelism with God's revealed will and character constitutes a sin, and at once makes us guilty in God's sight.[14]

He noted that this condition is a universal one, a

> vast moral disease which affects the whole human race, of every rank, and class, and name, and nation, and people, and tongue; a disease from which there never was but one [Jesus Christ] born of woman that was free.[15]

This disease, he said,

> pervades and runs through every part of our moral constitution and every faculty of our minds. The understanding, the affections, the reasoning powers, the will, are all more or less infected.[16]

Sin, then, is the absence of holiness, the antithesis of God's holiness. Sin is any human act or thought that contradicts or contravenes

God's being and God's will, expressed in God's word—his decree or law. To sin is to fall short—knowingly or unknowingly, willfully or negligently—of God's standard, of God's desire, of God's best ... of God. It is such a disastrous thing because sin stains us in a way that we ourselves cannot remove; it pains us and God and separates us from the God who is wholly holy.

This grieves God because he made us for intimacy with him. It grieves God because our sin ruins both ourselves and our environment, which he created as perfect and is pained to see destroyed. It grieves God because his holiness means he must judge sin and remove it, and in his righteous wrath, punishment must be meted out against the sinner. Sin brings separation from a holy God in this life, and it brings death and separation from God in eternity.

BIBLICAL SYNTAX

The Bible has a lot to say about sin, and we need to take note of its wisdom if we are going to know our enemy. Here is a list of Scriptures and the liberating truths they reveal:

- Sin is lawlessness (1 John 3:4).
- Sin is universal (Eccl. 7:20; John 8:7; 1 John 1:8).
- Sin affects all humankind through Adam's ancestry (Rom. 5:12).
- Sin looks for opportunities, crouching at our door (Gen. 4:7; Rom. 7:11).
- Sin follows the way of the Devil, the ruler of the kingdom of the air (Eph. 2:2).
- There are great sins (Ex. 32:21).

- There are lesser sins (1 John 5:16).
- Sin is against God (Ps. 51:4).
- Sin crushes the soul (Ps. 51:8).
- Sin separates us from God (Ps. 51:11).
- Sin separates us from glory (Rom. 3:23).
- Sin robs us of joy (Ps. 51:12).
- Sin is a power acting in and through us (Rom. 5:12, 21; 6:6; 1 Cor. 15:56).
- Sin is deceitful (Jer. 17:9).
- Sin is marked by craving (1 John 2:16).
- Sin is pleasurable (Heb. 11:25).
- Sin clings to us (Heb. 12:1).
- Sin grows (James 1:15).
- Sin brings death (Rom. 6:23; 8:10; 1 Cor. 15:56).
- The law highlights our sins (Rom. 3:20).
- God knows our secret sins (Ps. 90:8).
- God wants to remember our sins no more (Isa. 43:25).
- God can turn filthy sin as white as snow (Isa. 1:18).
- God's people awaited One who would bear their sins (Isa. 53).
- Jesus was so named because he would save men from their sins (Matt. 1:21).
- Jesus came into the world to save sinners (Matt. 9:13; 1 Tim. 1:15).
- Jesus Christ alone was sinless (1 John 3:5).
- Jesus ate with tax collectors and sinners (Mark 2:15–17).
- The cross is God's condemnation on sin (Rom. 8:3).

- Christ's blood cleanses us from every sin (1 John 1:7).
- Christ died for our sins (1 Cor. 15:3).
- The reason Jesus appeared was to take away our sins (1 John 3:5).
- Jesus was the propitiation for our sins (1 John 4:10).
- Grace triumphs over sin (Rom. 5:20).
- Forgiveness of sin is a gift of steadfast love and abounding mercy (Ps. 51:1).
- Sins can be passed over (Rom. 3:25), covered (Rom. 4:7), and removed (Rom. 11:27).
- In Christ we are dead to sin (Rom. 6:11).
- Heaven rejoices over sinners being saved (Luke 15:10).
- We are continually tempted to sin (Luke 17:1).
- We continue to struggle against sin (Heb. 12:4).
- Confession of sins brings forgiveness of sins (1 John 1:9).
- We must confess our sins to one another (James 5:16).
- We can grow in freedom from sin (1 John 3:1–10).
- We are to pray daily for the forgiveness of our trespasses (Luke 11:4).
- The church heralds the forgiveness of sins (Acts 2:38; 5:31; 10:43; 22:16).
- Heaven will be free of sin and sinners (Rev. 21).

WHERE DID IT ALL BEGIN?

The Bible doesn't attempt to answer every question we may have regarding sin; the origin of sin remains shrouded. The Western theological tradition generally says it is the absence of the good and of

God. Rather than a something, it is a lack of something, a privation, a negation, a vacuum left where humans have rejected God and his ways in their self-willing freedom.

God inspired and recorded in Scripture in narrative form the so-called "fall of Adam" to take us quite a way in understanding the nature and character and consequence of sin. This story presents the tragedy of human history, the opening of Pandora's box, the letting loose of hell. It is the very opposite of Darwin's thesis, for it is *the descent of man* from glory in Eden to bestiality in exile; it is the dark door opened that brought death and destruction and untold misery on the earth. All evil, suffering, pain, and misery may be laid at its feet.

And yet contained in its misery and curse, there is hope and promise. God and not Satan, hope and not despair, life and not death will have the last word. It is the story of protohumanity, and it is our story.

*The man and his wife were both naked, and they felt
no shame. (Gen. 2:25)*

This is the summary of the sublime bliss experienced on earth before sin entered Eden and humanity. Naked and shameless—perfect union, perfect harmony, perfect enjoyment between man and woman. No control, no self-interest, no guilt, no regrets, no shame. No covering but divine glory; nothing lewd, crude, or rude; nothing dirty, no one embarrassed. Here being naked carries a positive, affirming, embracing sense of innocence. There is no need for cover-up. All that will change, as every reference after this will convey the sense of exposure and guilt and corruption.

The word here for "no shame" is much stronger than "not embarrassed," conveying the sense of not being afraid or exploited or
vulnerable. But then all hell breaks loose, and paradise is well and
truly lost.

> *Now the serpent was more crafty than any of the wild
> animals the LORD God had made. (3:1)*

Suddenly there is a change of temperature—an ice-cold wind
blows across the warmth of the garden as the serpent creeps in.
Though Genesis does not state it as such, tradition understands
this serpent to be Satan, formerly an angel of light, appearing in
this form (and see Revelation 12:9). We are told the serpent was
created (the Lord made him) and craftier than all other animals.
The fact that this doorkeeper to darkness was created gives the lie
to any dualism. There is no equating of evil and good, no hint
that the demonic is an equal opposite to God … no balancing act
of yin and yang here. We are not told the serpent's name or his
origin, only about his character. We don't know where his capacity
to resist God's will came from, how evil came to be manifested in
the serpent, what his motivation was. It is presented as a fact of the
human couple's experience—one we all readily identify with. What
Scripture keeps covered, we do well not to explore too deeply.
Meanwhile, evil will enter the human race through Adam and Eve's
trusting in the serpent over God. God has no part in it.

The reference to "crafty" anticipates his twisting of Eve's mind
and God's word with half-truths and lies, innuendo and character
slurs. And so we are to understand sin as entering obliquely, as

has often been the case since then. Rarely is sin entertained and embraced head-on; it comes as a side wind, a strong hidden undercurrent. The demonic is subtle and shifty. This word *crafty* in verse 1 is *arum* in the Hebrew, where it sounds like the word in the previous verse (Gen. 2:25) for "naked," which is *arummim*. Before this, they were naked and without shame; after the crafty one comes, they are naked and ashamed. They will lose not just their innocence but their intimacy with God. And they will lose their lives.

> *He said to the woman, "Did God really say, 'You must*
> *not eat from any tree in the garden'?" (3:1)*

Here begins the serpent's defamation of God, which leads to his temptation of Eve. Was she unwise to even engage this serpent in conversation? We would say so now, but without previous experience or divine command, she could not know! The words of the serpent call into question God's command, attempting to subvert God's gracious provision and subtly sowing thoughts of God as mean and withholding rather than as the generous God who says they can eat fruit from almost everything. God had actually decreed that they could *freely* eat fruit from every tree in the garden—except one (Gen. 2:16–17). The serpent turns the statement of gracious provision—"eat all bar one"—into a restrictive prohibition—"eat not one." Sin begins with questioning God's goodness and the legitimacy of his decrees and then moves on to offer something "better."

Throughout Genesis 2, God is repeatedly referred to as the Lord God, *Yahweh Elohim,* but the serpent simply refers to him as God (*Elohim*), using just the abstract name for divinity, not the personal covenant name. This serpent is outside the intimate relationship experienced by those in the garden! His initial reference to Yahweh as just "God" should perhaps have rung alarm bells with Eve, warning her that this snake does not know her Lord God. Sin always attempts to remove Lord from God.

> *The woman said to the serpent, "We may eat fruit from the trees in the garden, but God did say, 'You must not eat fruit from the tree that is in the middle of the garden, and you must not touch it, or you will die.'" (3:2–3)*

Not only is there a difference between what God said and what the serpent claimed God had said, but there is also a notable difference between what God said and what Eve claims God said, for she fails to reflect the content and the tone of God's provision. God said they might freely eat from any of the trees, whereas the woman quotes God as merely saying they "may eat fruit from the trees"—her words do not reflect God's generosity encouraging her to eat to her heart's content. Already God's good provision is whittled down. She then appears to add to God's prohibition by saying, "And you must not touch it," a command God never gave, a command that adds to God's command, making God sound petty. By putting words in God's mouth, she appears already to "[have] moved slightly away from God toward the serpent's attitude."[17] Has sin entered at this point of exaggeration, or is this just the crafty spin of the serpent bringing confusion?

"You will not surely die," the serpent said to the
woman. *(v. 4)*

The Evil One sees she has taken the bait. No longer is this an
oblique, tangential questioning probe on God; now it's a direct fron-
tal assault—the Liar lies and says that God is a liar—"Death won't
come; instead, divinity will come. God has given this prohibition
because he is mean, because he is afraid, because he wants all the
glory to himself. What God said is not true." Sin blasphemes. Sin
always attacks God. It makes out that God's word is not truthful,
his ways are not good, he withholds the best from us, and he is self-
interested and miserly. The fact is, the demonic projects onto God
its own nature!

*For God knows that when you eat of it your eyes will
be opened, and you will be like God, knowing good
and evil. (v. 5)*

The serpent promises that the repercussions will not be damaging
but positive. Eve and Adam will not die; they will be divine—knowing good from evil. This is a lie. While to know good from evil is a
divine prerogative, it is also open to creatures, not least the serpent
himself; and yes, they would die—admittedly not immediately, but
sooner or later their disobedience would bring death. Did Adam and
Eve even understand what the concepts of knowing good and evil
meant? I don't think that was the offer that enticed Eve; I think it was
the offer that the gap between creature and Creator might be closed
by eating the fruit, sharing the knowledge, and being "like God."

It is not so much the knowledge they want as this God-likeness. The knowledge of good and evil, whatever that might mean—and they had no real clue—is merely the means to divinization. They are already the crown of creation. They are already made in God's image and made for intimacy with him, since they walked in the cool of the day with God. They know God is God and they are not; now they are being offered, so they think, the chance to be like their Creator. Thus sin calls into question God's goodness, his truthfulness, his provision, and his essential difference from all he has made.

Why, oh, why didn't Eve say, "And who are you, and where do you come from, and how do you know, and why do you care, and what am I to you, and why do you hate God?" Her sin was sealed when she trusted the serpent over the Lord and let his words carry weight over God's.

> *When the woman saw that the fruit of the tree was good for food and pleasing to the eye, and also desirable for gaining wisdom, she took some and ate it. She also gave some to her husband, who was with her, and he ate it. (v. 6)*

Pleasing to the eye? Perhaps. But how would she know it was good for food? She'd never eaten it! How did she know it was desirable for wisdom—wisdom would have avoided it! The serpent and sin have worked their dark magic; Eve takes leave of her senses and pries open hell.

She does it freely, of her own volition—she is not sinned against; she does it willingly, excitedly. Nowhere does the serpent tell them to eat the fruit—he does not force sin into their mouths. But the temptation of hitherto hidden enjoyment and knowledge proves too much. They are free to crush that snake—they are given authority to "fill the earth and subdue it," ruling over every fish in the sea and bird in the air and every living creature that moves on the land (1:28). That means that there in that garden, the Devil in serpent form is subject to them. But sin enters when it is entertained—and rather than rule the snake, they allow the snake to rule them. Yes, sin's temptation is intense, but there is a way out. Eve, however, wants in.

The hosts of heaven hold their breath in shock as Eve looks, and takes, and partakes. Adam is not to be left out, so he eagerly joins in … and Eden's twin towers collapse. Satan begins to laugh, and darkness descends over the face of the earth—and I'm sure God wept. Adam says nothing, but he eats just the same—he is as guilty, if not more so, for Eve faced the scheming onslaught of the twister, whereas Adam was one step removed. He should have been able to see the game play. But he would not have his wife know what he doesn't, and so he simply takes from her hand what he knows is forbidden. As he does so, he curses all his descendants to death (Rom. 5:12; 1 Cor. 15:22).

Then the eyes of both of them were opened, and they realized they were naked; so they sewed fig leaves together and made coverings for themselves. (Gen. 3:7)

The serpent is right about one thing—their eyes are opened. But once they are opened, Adam and Eve see only horror. It was God's grace that had withheld this knowing.

The *when* of 3:6 is followed by a *then* of 3:7. The *then* of sin always follows the *when*—there are always consequences. They have what they wanted. They now know more than they need, more than is good for them. Disobeying God brings a shiver into Eden. From being naked and unashamed, they are now naked and ashamed. The glory that covered them has departed. Innocence and enjoyment have turned to shame.

Shame is the first mark of sin—that gnawing guilt that robs us of peace right down to our marrow. Then comes the cover-up, a futile attempt to hide the trace of sin. Fig leaves may be large, but they wither—they can never do the job. In many ways the cover-up makes no sense—they know each other's bodies, as does all of Eden! This act of external cover-up will never cover their internal screaming shame.

> *Then the man and his wife heard the sound of the LORD God as he was walking in the garden in the cool of the day, and they hid from the LORD God among the trees of the garden. But the LORD God called to the man, "Where are you?" (vv. 8–9)*

They have become fools, thinking they would be like God. But now they see that they do not meet him as equals. Now they are mere mortals. And so they hide. At least, they try—for who can hide from God? Three times in this verse we meet "the LORD God," no longer the mere "God," the impersonal, distant deity spoken of by the serpent and Eve, and we are reminded that here is the one and only covenant Lord. Sin causes us to forget exactly who we are dealing with, who this sin is really against.

As if hiding their bodies isn't enough, now they hide them-selves. With knowledge of good and evil, they now know firsthand evil from good. Fear has entered their souls. Why so afraid of God? Because disobedience brings judgment. And although the *when* of their eating is to be followed by the *then* of God's judgment, he does not come immediately; still gracious, he waits for their walk in the cool of the day. The midday heat, it seems, is no time for the burden of curses. What grace—God knows that sin has come, that death has come, and this is a day that evil has won; but he comes as usual, because he loves to come.

Only this day, his heart is ready to burst. But sin will not keep him away. He is ever the God moving toward humanity. In sin they moved away from God, yet in love God moves toward them. Their sinfulness before God's holiness does not negate his loving-kindness.

Where are you? (v. 9)

These are perhaps the most remarkable, beautiful, and mournful words of the whole story. This is a cry of God's heart—a cry of loss and dereliction. There is proximity as he draws near them in the garden, but there is no intimacy. His beloved friends have brought chaos on the universe and placed a chasm between him and them. For God knows exactly where they are—in time and space, still in the garden, now behind the bush. But as the good shepherd comes looking for his lost sheep, calling them by name, we see God display tenderness, not roughness; as Derek Kidner said, "He must draw rather than drive [them] out of hiding."[18]

"Where are you?" is a big question. We may also see it as the existential question posed by God to Adam and Eve and all their descendants—*what has become of you?* The whole of the rest of Scripture is God's response to that chaos and that chasm. And it's the continuation of the chain of passing the buck that began in Eden. As God confronts Adam and Eve, they pass the blame—Eve blames the serpent, Adam blames Eve, and so it goes on. Sin always passes the buck, always tries to dodge and dislodge responsibility. Even the serpent has spent millennia saying, "It was God's fault for allowing it in the first place."

Sin's curse goes on too. Disobedience still has a consequence. Just as they knew nakedness, shame, guilt, and fear, so those things are now our acquaintances too.

> *The LORD God said to the serpent … "He will crush*
> *your head, and you will strike his heel." (vv. 3:14–15)*

But there is hope. Although God pronounces judgment, even in that first curse there is a promise of salvation to come. The serpent will crawl on the ground, and he will finally be crushed by the off-spring of the woman. Here is an anticipation of Christ, whose heel the serpent will certainly strike, but who will utterly crush the Evil One at Calvary.

Then, with their own verdicts ringing in their ears, the couple is expelled—exiled from that beautiful Eden, from its orchards and rivers, forbidden to return, as they are driven east. The woman, Eve, will suffer pain in childbirth, and the husband will rule over her. Adam will work a cursed ground with the sweat of his brow and then return to the soil as the "dust" from which he came. Death will come to their offspring, and all their children will be touched by their crime.

Forever after, humankind will be sin's refugees, restless for a lost home. The garden of God's delights is guarded by cherubim. We may not easily return.

But all is not completely lost. Eden will accompany them. In Jewish thought, the tabernacle and the temple were modeled after Eden.[19] And one day, Christ will remove the flaming sword and open Eden up again to all who trust in him. Though this was a day when darkness reigned, God makes it clear that sin will not win in the end. Eve's seed will return to paradise, to heaven on earth, to union and communion with God.

Meanwhile God makes coverings for them out of animal skins (v. 21). The animals are slaughtered, blood is shed, skins cover Adam and Eve's nakedness, and their sin is "covered" by blood. And so this is the first instance in history of the atonement for sin that will be established through the sacrificial system God offered to his people, ultimately consummated in the covering of human sin by the shed blood of Jesus at the cross.

As they depart in shame from the garden, they do not go alone. God goes with them. For he stays in the story and in their lives. Sin does not have the last word. And the rest of Scripture is God's journey with humankind as he seeks to get them back to Eden.

LORD, HAVE MERCY

This is our history, but nowadays not everyone thinks they have sinned. In an interview in the *Sunday Telegraph,* an actress, looking back over her life, made this claim:

I have never done anything bad to anyone. Never. And that is one of the things I am proud of. I have never hurt anybody; I have never been vicious about anybody, never taken any drugs, never tricked anyone; on the contrary, I can say that many people have done harm to me.... I basically think that when one meets one's maker, if I do, there won't be anything that I've done that I need to be ashamed of. Nothing.[20]

Methinks the lady doth protest too much! The mark of sin is often self-deception, motivated by the ever-so-insistent ego. It was the great satirist Malcolm Muggeridge who, before becoming a Christian in his old age, and after giving himself deeply to many vices, observed: "Human depravity is at once the most empirically verifiable fact yet most staunchly resisted datum by our intellectuals."[21]

And, it would seem, also by our aging actresses!

To some who were confident of their own righteousness and looked down on everybody else, Jesus told this parable:

"Two men went up to the temple to pray, one a Pharisee and the other a tax collector. The Pharisee stood up and prayed about himself: 'God, I thank you that I am not like other men—robbers, evildoers, adulterers—or even like this tax collector. I fast twice a week and give a tenth of all I get.'

"But the tax collector stood at a distance. He would not even look up to heaven, but beat his breast and said, 'God, have mercy on me, a sinner.'

"I tell you that this man, rather than the other, went home justified before God. For everyone who exalts himself will be humbled, and he who humbles himself will be exalted." (Luke 18:9–14)

Sin is about the way things really are, and accepting that reality will open for us a window into God's amazing and unexpected grace.

Chapter 4
The Beckoning of the Holy

HOLINESS, SINFULNESS, AND LOVING-KINDNESS

We have considered the holiness of God and the sinfulness of humankind. God's holiness is his absolute purity, his otherness, his moral perfection. Human sinfulness is the universal failure to measure up to God's standard—both active and passive; it is our imperfection, found in our suppression of truth and our willful disobedience. Coming near the holy shows our sinfulness in stark relief. Holiness and sinfulness are polar opposites and mutually exclusive by definition. They repel each other—sin runs from the holy, while holiness must distance itself from sin, either by somehow covering it or by breaking out in righteous judgment against it.

If holiness was God's only word and way toward us, we would die instantly. But God who is holy is God who is love. When Israel went into battle, she praised God for the splendor of his holiness while singing, "Give thanks to the LORD, for his love endures forever"

(2 Chron. 20:21). God is perfect in both holiness and loving-kindness. And it is his love that compels him to repeatedly find a way to cover sin, to enable sinners to enter communion with him. We saw this when Adam hid from God in sin and shame, and God, far from moving away, moved toward Adam, covering his naked shame with the skin of animals—covering his sin with their blood.

Sin is a powerful word, dark and demonic, filled with chaos and corruption and death; but it is not the final word. Holy love seeks a way, and it makes a way, for sin to be covered and cleansed.

This holy love is most clearly demonstrated at Calvary, when, in holiness, God breaks out against sin and sinners by judging his willing Son for our sin. Holiness cannot be negated—it must punish sin—but God so loves the world that he sent his only Son to be the sacrifice and substitution for our sin, so that we might be forgiven and walk freely into his eternal embrace. The cross is the place and the means where holy God meets sinful man. God is uniquely holy; humankind is universally and utterly sinful. Sin wages war against God; God is always seeking terms for peace.

UNEARTHING OLD TREASURES

A recent renovation of one of Oxford's oldest libraries unearthed a fragment from a printing plate hidden beneath the floorboards. It was a plate from the King James Version of the Bible; the text was from Leviticus 19. It had probably not seen the light of day since the library was built and the floor laid in 1677.

Leviticus 19 details three categories of commands directed toward the Israelites' relationship to God, with one another, and with their environment. All the Levitical prescriptions and prohibitions are a commentary on the core theme of Leviticus, repeated in chapters 11, 19 and 20: "Be holy because I, the LORD your God, am holy" (19:2).

This command is the interpretive key to understanding the purpose of the various laws within the whole drama of God and his people: The God who is holy wants his people to be holy. This theme is central to our understanding of Scripture—of God and our relationship with him—yet tragically, as in the Oxford library, it has often gotten buried beneath the church floorboards, upon which shelves of religious books and words have been stacked for centuries, few of which equal it in beauty and importance.

BE HOLY AS I AM HOLY

Scripture repeats this specific command in almost identical form eight times in seven separate verses, making it one of the most repeated texts in the Bible. Five of these occur in the Old Testament, amid lists of commands about worship addressed specifically to Israel as she lived distinct among the nations, but the rest are found in the New Testament, in both Peter and, slightly modified, in the Gospels, uttered by Jesus. Clearly God is addressing and inviting the church today to be holy as he is holy.

R. C. Sproul rightly states that

> this special call to Israel was really not new. It did not begin with Moses or even with Abraham. The call to holiness was first given to Adam and Eve.... We were created in the image of God. To be God's image meant, among other things, that we were to mirror and reflect God's character. We were created

to shine forth to the world the holiness of God. This was the chief end of man.[1]

While many of the specific Levitical laws that relate to the worshipping community are fulfilled in Christ and annulled for the Christian, this comprehensive command remains.

Throughout Scripture, the emphasis is on our state of being rather than on action. The verb Scripture employs is the verb *to be*, rather than *to do*, because holiness is not simply about commands to comply with; it is about a state to live in. This is where the Pharisee in Luke 18 went wrong: He could claim that he fulfilled many of the laws—not robbing, not doing evil, not committing adultery, fasting and tithing—yet Jesus declared he was not righteous before God (v. 14).

In a similar manner, the rich young ruler who said he had kept all the commandments knew he did not have eternal life, and he went away sad when Jesus told him to sell all he had and give it to the poor (vv. 18–23). This wasn't even a specific commandment in the law. So we see that holiness is not the result of an accountant's approach to the law but a pursuit of a state of being (with reference to the laws). The goal is not so much "not doing wrong" or "must do right"; those actions may be part of the means, but the goal is *being like God*. Here are the verses:

- Leviticus 11:44—I am the LORD your God; consecrate yourselves and be holy, because I am holy.
- Leviticus 11:45—I am the LORD who brought you up out of Egypt to be your God; therefore be holy, because I am holy.

- Leviticus 19:2—Be holy because I, the LORD your God, am holy.
- Leviticus 20:7—Consecrate yourselves and be holy, because I am the LORD your God.
- Leviticus 20:26—You are to be holy to me because I, the LORD, am holy.
- Matthew 5:48—Be perfect, therefore, as your heavenly Father is perfect.
- 1 Peter 1:15–16—But just as he who called you is holy, so be holy in all you do; for it is written: "Be holy, because I am holy."

What does this extraordinary statement by God mean? How are we to understand it? For many, this will be heard or read as burdensome law—a dictate from God, who sets the benchmark so high that we are doomed to fail. Others will see it as an opportunity—a mountain to be climbed.

1. "Be holy as I am holy" is a gracious invitation.

The source of the command is the heart of God. The purpose of the command is to establish union and communion between God and his people. The command must be heard above all else as grace, as invitation, as a generous welcome. It is the extraordinary beckoning of God for us to be with him. It is a divine word that addresses us and through which, as George Herbert said, "Love bade me welcome."[2] It is God speaking through his prophets and priests, saying to those in their sin, "Come and join me." God's grace takes the initiative.

Because his holiness may not be modified, it is we who must come, we who must accommodate him, not he us. This statement is extraordinary in its inclusivity. God would have us as he is. Far from being exclusive and excluding, he makes room for us. Karl Barth spoke of this as "the command to cleave to grace"[3]—yes, it is prescriptive; yes, it is demanding; but it is the embrace of grace. What a privilege—God would have us as he is! What royal on any throne ever entertained the notion of sharing that status with his subjects? What prime minister or president ever wanted citizens to share in the high office? Not one, not ever. Yet God, the holy Creator of the world, would have those unholy creatures as he is, where he is.

It is the call to come higher, come closer. Alec Motyer said, "Holiness is the most intimately divine word the Bible possesses." And thus the call to be holy as he is holy is the call to the most intimate union with God. Imitation of God has intimacy with God as the goal.

2. "Be holy as I am holy" offers true hope for transformation.

How many times have we bemoaned our sinfulness, nakedness, and shame, knowing our best efforts are like filthy rags; knowing we cannot clothe ourselves acceptably for his presence; knowing with Peter that Jesus should remove himself from us, for we are sinful men and women? While many bury this knowing, others hunger for purity. Their hunger is for God, as they long to be made fit for his presence.

This verse promises that there is another possibility and that the longing of the human heart for God, despite its sinful condition, can

be fulfilled. Our fate is not that of an Icarus, who aims to fly to the
sun, only to have the wax that holds the feathers melt in the heat.
Yes, many have tried to get close to God, only to crash to earth in sin,
their best efforts proving futile. But here God says that we may come
near the blazing sun of his purity without either being consumed or
crashing to earth. Here is hope—"Be holy as I am holy" is an open
door into the heart of God. It says that our sin has not closed the
door on God, has not forever ruined the relationship; we can be with
him, even be like him.

3. "Be holy as I am holy" is a tall order.

Peter cited this text in the negative context of *not* being conformed to former evil desires when we lived in ignorance (1 Peter
1:14). Holiness means not living as we once lived, as sinners. But the
positive truth is that holiness is living like God! "Man's highest duty
is to imitate his creator"[4]—we are called to aim high, for a righteousness that exceeds the most righteous Pharisees (Matt. 5:20). I am not
to be as holy as my godly parents or my godly Christian mentors.
The standard is not human but divine—the divine Son, who became
human. I am not aiming at self-improvement of the human; I am
aiming at the benchmark of divinity.

Why is this? Because God cannot change. He is eternally, utterly
holy in his being, and if he would have me join him, then I must
be like him. Being holy is conforming one's thinking and actions to
God's nature and character. His holy character is revealed through
the covenant he established with his chosen people, Israel. The moral
aspect to this covenant is summarized in the Ten Commandments. To
be holy like God will result in conforming to his moral commands,

which reveal his character. And later we shall see that holiness is therefore the imitation of Christ.

Both the Old Testament and the New Testament repeat the call to be holy as God is holy. Why? Because

> the goal of both the old and the new covenants is the same—to create people who morally conform to God's character.[5]

4. "Be holy as I am holy" places responsibility on us, individually and corporately.

Holiness is not assigned and applied to us purely on the basis of God's command to "be holy." There is great blessing in the offer of holiness, but this is still a command. There is nothing passive about holiness—it won't come and find us if we wait long enough! This is something that requires action, energy, commitment, tenacity. When Moses recorded, "Be holy, because I am holy" (Lev. 11:45), he was defining the purpose and orientation of the whole of Old Testament Law, all 613 commands. When Jesus commanded, "Be perfect … as your heavenly Father is perfect" (Matt. 5:48), he was summarizing the whole of his Sermon on the Mount, which demonstrates and directs toward that perfection. Every Old Testament Jew was to apply himself or herself individually to Moses' commandments. Similarly, every New Testament disciple was to apply himself or herself to Jesus' instructions.

While this sounds very personal and individual—not least because we will each stand accountable before God's judgment seat as an individual—we must not forget the corporate dimension. The text in Leviticus 19:2 is prefaced by "Speak to the entire assembly."

Peter also addressed the whole church, commanding "be holy, because I am holy" to "obedient children" (plural) and speaking of them as a holy nation (1 Peter 1:16, 14; 2:9). So, while responsibility is placed on us to participate in this pathway to holiness, we do so as a holy people, a family of God's children working together to holiness. Holiness is a joint pursuit. Godlikeness, conformity to his character, is a pilgrimage, a journey made together. There is no individual pietism here—we are to walk and work with one another.

5. "Be holy as I am holy" is a command that comes to all of us.

Jerry Bridges rightly noted:

> God has called every Christian to a holy life. There are no exceptions to this call. It's not a call only to pastors, missionaries and a few dedicated Sunday school teachers.[6]

This call comes to the newest convert and the oldest saint. No one may attempt to evade its gaze; no one has a get-out clause. Nor, by contrast, may anyone feel too sinful to receive its gentle, gracious affirmation.

6. "Be holy as I am holy" is a call to safety.

Karl Barth noted that sin not only disturbs fellowship and makes it impossible, but sin before the holiness of God brings peril.[7] And so the call to absolute holiness is a call to safety—the privilege of being holy as God is holy is the antidote to the precarious predicament of sin as danger. Holiness is the only safe place to hide from God's holy judgment on sin, both now, in terms of this life, and in eternity. We hide from the holiness of God in the holiness of God.

7. "Be holy as I am holy" includes promise.

When Jesus said, "Be perfect, therefore, as your heavenly Father is perfect" (Matt. 5:48), he moved the emphasis from holiness to maturity. Now, both of these point to the same condition—blamelessness—but Jesus may have been introducing a welcome note of promise here. He used the verb *to be* in its future tense ("you will be"). This is usually translated as an imperative—"you are to be"—rather than its natural rendering as plain future tense. In fact, the Septuagint (the Greek translation of the Old Testament) also renders Leviticus 19:2 as a future rather than an imperative. Throughout the rest of the Sermon on the Mount, Jesus used clear imperatives. So why did he move to a future here? It is perfectly possible to see Jesus' statement not as command but as promise.

Jesus had given the list of new commandments, many more stringent than those given by Moses and no doubt drawing a groan from his hearers, who felt utterly unable to comply. But amid these laws, he offered this hope: "One day you will be perfect. One day, because of grace, you will be perfect as your heavenly Father is perfect." Whether this future tense was intended, we cannot be sure, but it certainly is true—eschatologically, in the twinkling of an eye, we *shall* be like him, holy as he is holy, for we shall see him as he is (1 John 3:2). This promise fuels greater resolve on our part, and so John immediately continued, "Everyone who has this hope in him purifies himself" (v. 3).

HOLY PERFECTION—AN IMPOSSIBLE DREAM?

Most of us have experienced times when with all our heart, soul, and strength we longed to be holy as God is holy—to be like Christ, to walk as he walked, to live as he lived, to be free from the besetting sins, transformed into his likeness by the Spirit. But for most of us, that is not the all-consuming passion that defines us day in and day out, and so we are not actually surprised when we fall short. We probably dedicate only some percentage of our being some of the time to the pursuit of holiness. But what if we were to give 100 percent? Would we, could we ever really, in this life, be holy as God is holy?

Clearly we don't ever stop being creatures before the Creator. Being like God does not mean being God but rather being restored to our full, unfallen image of God. But is it really possible to be as perfect and holy a creature as God is perfect and holy a Creator? Can we ever expect to attain the perfection that Jesus asks of us, that parity with the being of God whereby we attain moral sinlessness? I asked several members of my church staff. They all concluded *no*. But had they set the bar too low and settled for too little?

This issue of whether holy perfection is attainable in this life is not a new one. It is an ancient debate that was played out between the British bishop Pelagius and the African bishop Augustine. In the late fourth and early fifth centuries, as theological orthodoxy was being cemented, one issue that caused these men to lock horns was whether it was possible for man to live a sinless, perfect life.

Augustine was developing an influence through his treatment of the original sin in the garden of Eden, imputed to each and every human being (except Christ) at conception and leaving an irremovable inclination toward evil. Augustine described man as a lump of sin unable to make any move to save himself apart from a preemptive move of God's grace.[8] Augustine famously prayed, "Command what you will, but give what you command," seeing that grace alone could enable the sinner to reach the standard God set. This pained Pelagius, who, as J. N. D. Kelly said, was

> primarily a moralist, concerned for right conduct and shocked by what he considered demoralizing pessimistic views of what could be expected of human nature. The assumption man could not help sinning seemed to him an insult to his Creator.[9]

Pelagius quoted the commands of God through Moses and Peter to "be holy as I am holy" and of Christ to "be perfect as your heavenly Father is perfect" as proof that a man could, if he so willed, observe God's commands without sinning. He said that these commands were meaningless if that were not possible. Rejecting any concept of original conception in sin, Pelagius argued that the judgment of sin would only be just if man had the capacity not to sin. He claimed that the command or call to perfection is a pointless untruth if it can't be attained, and he did not believe God would set a standard he knew we would all fail. Pelagius believed that all human beings, not just those redeemed, were free to exercise their will and choose to do good by virtue of their God-given nature. This perfect coherence with God's will was attainable and proven, he suggested, by the sinless lives of Abel,

Enoch, Joseph, and Job. This perfect state could not, he suggested, be attained once and for all, never to be forfeited, but needed to be maintained by strenuous and steady application.[10]

While commending Pelagius's recognition of the "wonderful privileges" and "high destiny" God has given to humanity, Kelly clearly pointed out that Pelagius's view was defective through its failure to recognize human weakness.[11] Pelagius simply didn't take seriously the depth of our sin and its stranglehold on humanity. He was declared a heretic by the bishop of Rome in 417 and outlawed as such by the Ecumenical Council of Ephesus in 431.

While Augustine vehemently challenged Pelagius's notion that any person, of his or her own free will, may attain perfection without the aid of divine grace, he did appear to leave open the possibility of a person attaining it in grace. So he stated the biblical imperative of perfection (Deut. 18:13; Matt. 5:48; 2 Cor. 13:11; Eph. 1:4; Col. 1:28), enjoining us to "hold on to the course of perfection," albeit freely admitting, "Who may be said to walk without spot damnable and venial sins?"—the assumed answer being, "No one!"[12]

NOT HALF A CHRISTIAN

Perhaps the greatest advocate of the ability to attain to a sinless perfection and so comply with the commandment "Be perfect as your heavenly Father is perfect" was the great revivalist and reformer John Wesley. He famously developed his doctrine of Christian perfection, sometimes called being "perfect in love" or "entire sanctification." As a young man at Oxford University, Wesley was burdened by sin and matters of personal holiness. He began the famous "Holy Club," which met just a few hundred yards from the study where I now write. There the members committed themselves to rigorous spiritual exercises—daily offices, confessions, fasting, and ministry to the poor. Wesley was always an admirer of William Law (Law by name, law by nature), who produced several works on the holy life and perfection, notably *A Serious Call to a Devout and Holy Life.*

Wesley had a lifelong desire for holiness. He realized all his best efforts didn't produce it. Though he never claimed to attain it personally, he came to develop a doctrine in which entire sanctification—Christian perfection—was construed to be an experience within the reach of mortal man. In his collected works on the matter,[13] often autobiographical and personal, he detailed how he became convinced of "the absolute impossibility of being half a Christian" and determined, through God's grace, to be completely devoted to him. He noted:

On June 25th 1744—1st Conference [at which he gathered his ministers and preachers]: seriously considered the doctrine of Sanctification or Perfection.

~Question: What is it to be sanctified? Answer: To be renewed in the image of God in righteousness and true holiness.

~Question: What is implied in being a perfect Christian? Answer: Loving God with all our heart and mind and soul.

~Question: Does this imply that all inward sin is taken away? Answer: Undoubtedly—or how can we be said to be 'saved from all our uncleannesses' Ezekiel 36:29?

This theme was revisited at the second conference in August of the following year:

~Question: When does inward sanctification begin? Answer: In the moment a man is justified. (Yet sin remains in him yea, the seed of all sin, till he is sanctified throughout.) From that time a believer gradually dies to sin and grows in grace.

~Question: Is this ordinarily given till a little before death? Answer: It is not, to those who expect it sooner.

~Question: But may we expect it sooner? Answer: Why not? Although we grant (1) the generality of believers are not sanctified till near death, (2) few of those to whom Paul wrote his epistles were at that time, (3) nor Paul himself at the time of writing his epistles…that does not prove that we may not be so today!

~Question: In what manner should we preach sanctification? Answer: Always by the way of prom-ise—of drawing rather than driving.[14]

How was Wesley's view different from that of Pelagius? Both appealed to the same mandate in Scripture; both claimed the same possible end result. Yet they were different because of the means. Pelagius thought one could achieve sanctification by one's effort alone, through pure self-willing. Wesley was clear it was a partnership with the Holy Spirit, a work of grace, and a spiritual experience in which perfection was infused. Wesley emphasized that the mark of perfection was conformity to the law, summed up by Jesus as "loving God with all our heart, soul and strength and loving our neighbor as ourselves."[15] Consequently, this experience was sometimes called "perfect love" (1 John 4:18), whereby we are perfected in our love for God and man. This experience is that which awaits all believers at death, but some may enter it beforehand. Wesley recognized that few attained it, even Paul himself, but he urged us on to it. Wesley believed that this state of perfection, which came by attending oneself to grace, did not make one free from temptation to sin or from culpable acts of the flesh. It was not a state of being unable to sin but rather of choosing not to sin.

This doctrine has become a mainstay of the Wesleyan holiness movement, which became very powerful in the nineteenth-century American church. They believed, as Paul Bassett stated in a standard reference work on Wesleyan holiness, that

> just as there is a distinct, identifiable time at which one is born or one dies, so there is such a moment in which the spiritual cleansing/filling Work is done. This moment of spiritual cleansing and

filling fundamentally reconstitutes our relationship with God and others, and opens up a moment by moment process of growth and grace and of demonstrations of the fruit of the Holy Spirit.[16]

The experience of entire sanctification opens the door to the state of perfection—

God's ridding the believer of all that is morally unlike himself and reception of the unqualified unconditional love of God.[17]

This is a gift of cleansing received by faith, and that faith is itself a gift, but one available to all who choose to accept it at any time.

In late-nineteenth-century America, this belief in an instantaneous reception of perfection came to be interpreted as what Jesus and the apostles called "the baptism of the Holy Spirit." Within the holiness movement many began to seek this experience in order that they might become perfected. It gave rise to the so-called "Pentecostal" movement, which, while gaining the so-called "baptism," failed to gain the so-called "perfection." Quickly, this experience then became reinterpreted as a baptism of spiritual "power" rather than moral "perfection."

But is it attainable? Can I be perfect? J. Rodman Williams claimed that the doctrine of entire sanctification in its Wesleyan presentation "is neither biblically sound nor experientially valid."[18] I am inclined to agree that a one-off encounter with the Spirit will not perfect me. I have had many notable encounters with God by his Spirit, and the wrestle for purity continues. I know many other sincere, wonderful Christians who have been filled with the Holy Spirit, yet not one would claim to be perfect as their heavenly Father is perfect; and even if they did, I would have to question the evidence!

The Old Testament command in Leviticus to "be holy as God is holy" is framed by the instructions on sacrifices for sin. Presumably God didn't expect them to fulfill his command and graciously provided the means for forgiveness when they fell short of perfection. Similarly, Donald Hagner noted that, while Jesus sets the moral standard high, demanding perfection, he realistically provides us shortly thereafter with a daily petition in the Lord's Prayer: "Forgive us our sins, for we also forgive everyone who sins against us" (Luke 11:4). He said,

> The fact that we are to pray regularly for such forgiveness indicates that, at least for the present, sin unfortunately will remain a reality in the life of the disciples.[19]

Among the most balanced treatments of this theme is that of Ralph Martin, the Roman Catholic scholar, in his classic study on holiness, *The Fulfillment of All Desire*. Commenting on Christ's command to be perfect, he said that when we hear such words, we can be tempted to discouragement and even failure if left to our own resources. However, he pointed out that Christ also said, "What is impossible with men is possible with God" (Luke 18:27).[20] Martin then summarized Pope John Paul II's teaching on the matter, noting in strong Reformed tone that

> Union with God of this depth is totally unattain-
> able by our own effort; it is a gift that only God
> can give; we are totally dependent on His grace for
> progress in the spiritual life.... God is eager to give
> us this grace and bring us to deep union.... At the
> same time our effort is indispensable. Our effort is
> not sufficient to bring about such union, but it is
> necessary.[21]

Martin concluded that such effort is "*infinitely* worth it."[22]

Christians are people who know they cannot make themselves perfect, who know they cannot fulfill the moral commands of God (even out of the correct motive of loving God and neighbor) by their own efforts; and so they look to Christ to forgive their failure; they look to Christ as the example of perfection; and they look to the Spirit to work and walk out Christ's perfection in them.

Dietrich Bonhoeffer once said, "The hall-mark of the Christian is the 'extraordinary.'"[23] What a glorious goal—conformity to Christ, perfection of my being, holiness as he is holy. It is something unattainable without divine grace and unattainable without human determination. Put them together, and we are getting somewhere! God's longing for union with us, his provisions of grace to us, and our passionate pursuit after holiness will get us on the journey.

It has been said, "Aim for the sun, and you'll hit the moon; aim for the moon, and you won't break the atmosphere." Many aim too low and don't get near. Moses, Christ, Paul—all encouraged us to aim for the top, to aim for perfection. To aim for character utterly conformed to God's holiness. God did not decree that goal so that we would be disappointed and constantly frustrated. As is often the case in mountain climbing, the nearer we get to the top, the more we clearly see how far we have yet to go. But we press on. A. W. Tozer said, "Every man is as holy as he really wants to be."[24] This side of eternity we will never fully bring our whole being into absolute permanent conformity with God's desire that we be holy as he is holy; and so entire perfection may be known only momentarily (when we're asleep?!). But what an amazing thing to live for!

In the classic movie version of Don Quixote, *Man of La Mancha*, there is a song that makes sense of the knight's errand. Many think him mad, his song but the extensions of senility. But he feels driven by a noble destiny. The song is not written from a Christian viewpoint, but it's a glorious challenge if we take it up sincerely in our call from the perfect, holy God to be perfectly holy. One notable verse challenges:

> This is my quest, to follow that star,
> No matter how hopeless, no matter how far.[25]

The quest for holiness may be following a far-off star, but it's not a hopeless journey. Even as the wise men set off following their star to the One born to be King, we, too, can follow "that star" on the journey to the likeness of Christ.

Chapter 5
Unholy Religion

RED COATS BANNED

She walked into my early morning student communion service wearing a bright red mackintosh. It looked fantastic. She looked fantastic. "That is an incredible coat you've got there," I told her. And others agreed. "Thanks," said the shy young postgraduate. "I bought it for myself—at my old church, girls were not allowed to wear red; we were told it inflamed the passions of the men."

No, this was not the Taliban ban on red for the ladies—this was a case of the modern-day Christian evangelical Pharisee calling a glorious, God-created, life-affirming color *bad,* toning down the "scarlet" in women, bringing control, fear, guilt, and condemnation in the name of religion!

In the last chapter, we considered the most extravagant invitation ever sent out: "Be holy as I am holy"; or, as Jesus put it, "Be perfect as your heavenly Father is perfect." This divine welcome, among the most directly repeated statements in Scripture, is the design of God, who, since the time of creation, has desired that he and we might be with and for each other. The whole narrative of Scripture may be seen as a commentary on this call: God's description of it, God's provision of it, man's rejection or deviation from it, God's correction, and the ultimate perfection of it in the new heaven and earth. Gerard Hughes rightly noted: "The call to holiness is the echo of God's longing for each of us."[1] *Holy* is an intimate word; holiness is lovers' language. Theologian Ralph Martin said,

> To be holy is not primarily a matter of … how much
> Christian activity we're engaged in; it's a matter of
> having our heart transformed into a heart of love.[2]

Holiness is conforming our lives to God's will—not as subservient creatures before their Creator, not as soldiers before their commanding officer, but as sons and daughters and lovers of God. As we have said before, holiness is loving God with all our heart, soul, and strength, and loving our neighbor as ourselves. The highway of holiness will involve certain appropriate dos and don'ts—but the motive, the goal, is union and communion with God. Holiness is about companionship with the divine. To be holy is to be fully alive, fully human, whole, as God intended.

THE BENCHMARK OF HOLINESS

> We were talking about cats and dogs the other day
> and decided that both have consciences but the

dog, being an honest, humble person, always has
a bad one, but the cat is a Pharisee and always
has a good one. When he sits and stares you out
of countenance he is thanking God that he is not
as these dogs, or these humans, or even as these
other cats.[3]

The Pharisees were a holiness sect. New Testament scholar
Dietrich Müller said that, by the time of Christ, the Pharisees were
"the most respected leading religious group in Judaism."[4] The Pharisees
were held by others—and certainly by themselves—as the benchmark
of holiness in the time of Christ. Ask any first-century Jew, "Who is
holy?" and they would undoubtedly say, "The Pharisees." Ask them
what holiness meant, and they would say, "Washing, separating, tithing." The mark of their religion of "holiness" was an excessive exercise
of cleanliness laws, turning obsessive-compulsive hygiene disorder into
religious virtue.

The origins of the Pharisees remain unclear, but they came
to prominence in the second century BC, during the time of
the Maccabean Revolt. Their forerunners are mentioned in the
Apocrypha (1 Maccabees 2:42; 7:13; 2 Maccabees 14:6) where they
are spoken of as mighty men of Israel who were devoted to the law.
These were the "Hasidim" (from a Hebrew word meaning "piety,"
based on the Hebrew root word *chesed,* meaning "loving-kindness").
They developed into different branches with different focuses—
a violent revolutionary group opposed to the "unclean Roman
occupation" and the group devoted to studying Torah, the Law of
God.[5] Josephus, himself a Pharisee, spoke of this group as adherents

to a "philosophy"—they were an intellectual group. After the fall of Jerusalem and the destruction of the temple, the study of Torah became the dominant mark of the tradition influencing Judaism. Modern-day Hasidic Jews are, in many respects, descendants of the Pharisees, both in ideology and in spirituality.

Their nickname was "the Holy Community of Jerusalem." Their founding fathers divided their waking day into one-third study, one-third prayer, and one-third manual work.[6] They were a strict, closed society with numbers somewhere around six thousand—about a third the number of the priests and Levites. Their number did not generally include Levites, but they sought to adhere to the same or even more demanding laws of purity. The word Pharisee (*pharisaoi* in the Greek) comes from the Hebrew *perushim,* which at root means "to divide or separate." Pharisees were separatists.[7]

They were not a ruling class—they had no direct access to power—but they took an interest in politics, driven by their wider goals of seeing Israel as a holy nation genuinely achieved. Because of their religious scruples, they were rarely in direct power—close relationships with the Romans would inevitably lead to compromise on their core values of purity and separation. However, they were always influencing politics, as we see in their manipulations and machinations with the Herodians, Sanhedrin, and high priest. Their contemporaries the Essenes, another holiness cult, perceived temple religion to be so compromised and corrupted that they withdrew from society to the desert at Qumran to found a community based on purity. By contrast, the Pharisees sought to pursue holiness and separation *within* society and so transform that society.

James Dunn said their aim was to extend temple religion of purity throughout the whole of Israel, making the whole land effectively the temple—holy, set apart in unbroken continuum.[8]

The theological underpinning to their whole way of life was the holiness of God, the God who had called Israel to be holy. In the Torah, God had laid out the mark of holiness, how holiness could be maintained and the people kept in covenant. Ritual purity in particular was seen as a core expression of holiness.[9]

The Pharisees were often spoken of in the same breath as the scribes. No mere copyists, the scribes were the lettered, intellectual, professional doctors of theology (Luke 5:17) who interpreted the law and converted it to practical principles that the Pharisees sought to adhere to so they could attain or maintain purity. Together, the scribes and Pharisees developed a sophisticated system of application of Torah, and these interpretations and applications of the law became as binding as the biblical tradition. Indeed, the famous Rabbi Shammai, born a generation or so before Christ, declared there were in fact two Torah: the written Torah and the oral Torah.[10] He regarded both as of equal authority.

The Pharisees were formed into regional assemblies with their own leaders, each following their own emphasis of a respected rabbi (a teacher of the law). Membership of the association came after a lengthy period of trial, upwards of a year, during which each probationer had to have followed rigorous hygiene and dietary laws, not allowing any garment to be unclean through contact with anyone or anything Levitically impure.

It has been suggested that there were three core expressions of their religion: meals, Sabbath observance, and tithing:

> The preparation of food as well as their meal-time companions were carefully controlled to avoid impurity through non-observance of the food rules or contact with people likely to be impure.[11]

Strict Sabbath observance meant avoiding anything designated as work, which would violate the day of rest. The scribes developed a whole series of prescriptions and prohibitions detailing what was and wasn't work on a Sabbath.

Tithing became a core expression of holiness, precisely because this was one area where it was possible to be tempted to be nonobservant and no one would be the wiser, not knowing your income or your giving.

These three core expressions of holiness became focal points for tension with Jesus: mealtimes, yet Jesus ate with tax collectors and sinners; Sabbath observance, yet Jesus healed the sick on the Sabbath and even allowed his disciples to pick ears of corn; tithing, yet Jesus rebuked them for neglecting the weightier matters of the law.

TWO VERSIONS OF HOLINESS

The Pharisees were a central part of religious Jewish society and are a significant feature in gospel literature. Matthew and Luke each refer to them twenty-seven times, Mark another twelve, and John nineteen. They are the main antagonists of Christ in the Gospels.

The Pharisees' casuistic interpretation of the law led them to a self-righteous and self-deceiving view of truth. Christ suddenly shattered their belief in their own holiness and the esteem that all held them in. The sustained clash between them and Jesus was not about whether it was right to pursue holiness but about the nature of holiness and the way to it. The meaning and the means of holiness were the points of conflict.

It soon became clear that Jesus was advocating a very different kind of holiness; and in so doing, he was undermining the very pillars on which their whole devotion to God and pursuit of purity rested. Jesus seemed to them a violent iconoclast, smashing underfoot everything they held dear. Both of them sought to fulfill the law, but Jesus attacked the Pharisees' scribal tradition of interpretation (called *halakah*), which had added to the Torah layer upon layer of demand, nuance, prescription, and application. Jesus regarded all this as mere "traditions of men" that obscured the truth (Mark 7:8). At times, he brusquely pulled down these Babels to get to the heart of the matter, the spirit behind the law.

We don't have enough space here to give a detailed commentary, but let's take a look at the main interactions between the Pharisees and Jesus in the Gospels.

The first mention we have of the Pharisees is when they come to check out John the Baptist. He is quick and sharp, denouncing them as a brood of vipers and commanding them to produce fruit in keeping with repentance. He warns them that claiming ancestry to Abraham carries no weight with God and that ax and fire will come against whatever does not bear fruit, including them (Matt. 3:7–10).

Jesus begins his discourse on righteousness by raising the standard above that which was generally regarded as the heights of holiness, saying that unless the righteousness of his listeners surpassed that of the Pharisees, they would not enter the kingdom of heaven—and neither, presumably, would the Pharisees (Matt. 5:20).

Jesus has thrown down the gauntlet. The Pharisees pick it up. If Jesus is so righteous, why does he recline and eat with tax collectors and sinners, something a Pharisee seeking purity would never do (Matt. 9:11)? Jesus replies that it is not the healthy who need a doctor but the sick; he has not come to call the righteous but sinners to repentance (9:12–13). The Pharisees might well have accepted this, as it implied that the sinners were sick and unsaved—and even potentially that the Pharisees were the righteous. However, Jesus also adds that they need to learn what God meant when he said, "I desire mercy, not sacrifice"—a stinging rebuke from Hosea 6:6 against the self-righteous religious whose sacrifices were no substitute for the true religion shown in compassion.

Next, their commitment to cleanliness and food hygiene is disturbed when they see Jesus' disciples eating without first following the ritual washings for purification. So they ask Jesus why he does not make his disciples follow the traditions of the elders, who have commanded washing first (Matt. 15:1–2). Jesus responds by asking the Pharisees why they have broken the commandment of God for the sake of tradition—not honoring their mothers and fathers as they try to impress God through giving offerings of money or time that they should have spent looking after their parents. Jesus then follows up with a fierce attack, calling them the hypocrites of whom Isaiah prophesied: "These people honor me with their lips, but their hearts are far from me. They worship me in vain; their teachings are but rules taught by men" (Matt. 15:7–9).

Jesus continues by addressing the Pharisees' pet theme of hygiene, saying that "it is not what goes into the mouth that defiles a person, but what comes out of the mouth; this defiles a person"

(15:11 ESV). Jesus seems to be undermining one of the mainstays of their religious identity and purity: what you eat and how you eat. The Pharisees take offense—as well they might, since Jesus is clearly implying that these Pharisees, who thought themselves ritually clean, are actually filthy inside.

They are incensed when they see Jesus' disciples picking ears of grain on the Sabbath and rebuke Jesus for allowing his followers to violate the traditional interpretation of the command to keep the Sabbath day holy (12:1–8). Jesus answers them with a precedent from Scripture: David ate the consecrated bread from God's house when he was hungry; this showed that satisfying hunger is a legitimate concern over narrow conformity to law. Jesus again quotes Hosea 6:6 at them, saying they need to learn the meaning of "I desire mercy, not sacrifice" (Matt. 12:7). Jesus concludes this skirmish by stating that "the Son of Man is Lord of the Sabbath," asserting his lordship and sovereign right to interpret Scripture and apply the law (12:8).

Jesus goes on to a synagogue and gives further insight into what is legitimate on the Sabbath. He poses the question, Is it legitimate to heal and do good on the Sabbath? He then confirms the answer by healing a man with a withered hand. What happens next is crucial— rather than accept Jesus' interpretation of what constitutes work on the Sabbath and stand in awe at his power, the Pharisees go out and conspire against him.

The Pharisees, it seems, have made up their minds about Jesus and rejected him as a false prophet. When confronted by the clear evidence of power flowing through Christ, they are offended; even worse, when they see him exorcise demons, they come perilously close to committing the unforgivable sin—they ascribe his power to the demonic, saying it is by Beelzebub, the prince of demons, that he casts them out (Matt. 9:34; 12:24). Nevertheless, twice they ask Jesus to offer a sign to legitimate his claim that he is sent from God. Both times Jesus replies that "a wicked and adulterous generation asks for a ... sign" and that the only sign they will be given is the sign of Jonah (12:39). Jonah, of course, was buried in the sea for three days, but they are left to figure that one out for themselves.

COLLISION COURSE

Jesus specifically warned his followers against what he termed the "yeast" of the Pharisees. In Jewish understanding, yeast was unclean. Jesus employed a negative analogy for how something very small but corrupt (yeast), if mixed into something larger and good (dough), can defile the lot. Analogously, the Pharisees' spirit and instruction and application of the law (not the law itself) could influence the whole batch of true religion and make it unclean (Matt. 16:6–12). The Pharisees were continually trying to test Jesus on his theology to see if he was sound. They came to him on traditional rabbinic debates like the legitimacy of divorce (19:3), the question of what was the greatest commandment (22:35–37), and the concern of when the kingdom would come (Luke 17:20). Sometimes they were simply setting a trap for him in order to have him condemned, as when they asked him whether taxes should be paid to Caesar (Matt. 22:17) or when they brought a woman caught in adultery and asked whether she should be stoned according to the law (John 8:1–11). This second example shows that they understood Jesus was compassionate and merciful, and they expected him to want to let her go and so violate the law, which said she should be stoned! Ironically, his answer led them to leave and let her go—thus making *them* the lawbreakers in this instance.

The Pharisees tested Jesus, but at times he tested them. When he asked them whose son the Christ was, they replied, "David's"—so he made them look less than brilliant by asking how the Messiah can be a son of David while David calls him Lord (Matt. 22:41–45). Again, he asked them whether John the Baptist was sent from God. This time cowardice kept them from answering: Even though they believed John to be a false prophet, they didn't want to upset the crowd, who had embraced the Baptist (21:25–26).

As things between Jesus and the Pharisees became completely polarized, Jesus told parables against them, representing them as the farming tenants who refused to give the fruit to the owner, beat the owner's servants, and finally killed the owner's son (21:33–46). They knew Jesus was speaking about them, accusing them of thieving from God and abusing God's prophets. Jesus even prophesied his own death (as the master's son) at their hands.

It would not be long before the plot to have him killed was put into effect. They were there at his arrest (John 18:3) and were there to petition Pilate to guard the tomb after his death (Matt. 27:62). They were there as the church was birthed, arresting and punishing the apostles, chasing them from city to city and inciting trouble against them.

We have focused on Matthew's gospel. The others tell us a little more. Mark tells us that the Pharisees plotted with the Herodians to kill Jesus (3:6), although Luke relates that they quite duplicitously told Jesus to leave, saying the Herodians were after him (13:31). Luke says they "loved money" (16:14) and also tells the story of the

Pharisee and the tax collector, in which the Pharisee applauds himself before God for his religious tithing, fasting, and righteous living, while the notorious sinner beats his chest and begs for mercy. Jesus says that the tax collector and not the Pharisee went away "justified before God"—pronounced righteous (18:10–14).

Westerholm noted,

> In proclaiming to Israel the dawning of the reign of God, Jesus demanded a response quite different from that sought by the Pharisees, who summoned the nation to adhere to Torah's laws as interpreted by Pharisaic scribes.[12]

Consequently, and tragically, as Müller said,

> Their understanding of God and their resultant understanding of the law made the Pharisees blind to the true offer and claim of God meeting them in Jesus.[13]

WOE! WHOA! NOT THE WAY TO GO!

Matthew 23 is the most sustained reflection on the Pharisees in Scripture and gets us to the heart of their religion and Christ's opinion of it. It is his relentless assault against their form of holiness, and no doubt hearing it exacerbated the Pharisees' intent to remove Jesus once and for all. Many have seen a contrast between the seven woes against the Pharisees and their false discipleship and the seven beatitudes offered in the Sermon on the Mount defining true discipleship.

We are being shown two religious ways to live—one that leads to spiritual life and another that leads to spiritual death. Davies and Allison pointed out that the seven woes against the Pharisees initially focus on scribal disagreements over interpreting the law, but they end with reference to the murder of the prophets. This mirrors exactly the plot of the gospel and Christ's relations with the Pharisees—which begins with disagreement over the law and ends with them killing Jesus.[14]

Doubtless Jesus did not have every single individual Pharisee in mind when he made these statements. We know that Nicodemus was a Pharisee who was drawn to Jesus and even defended him. The diatribe in Matthew 23 is aimed more at the overall direction and expression of the movement, which focused religion on externals and failed to discern God's priorities—indeed, it failed to discern God come in Christ.[15] Müller rightly said,

> In Pharisaism Israel strove for true faith and obedience to God but had become totally hardened in formalism and barred itself from precisely that for which it was searching—to please God.[16]

Matthew 23's treatment of the Pharisees is divided into two sections. In verses 1–12, Jesus warns the people not to imitate the Pharisees; and in verses 13–32, he pronounces woes on the Pharisees. Let us summarize what Jesus says about their religion:

- Pharisees teach the Law of Moses, and that Law must be respected. (vv. 2–3)

- Pharisees must not be imitated—they don't practice what they preach. (v. 3)
- Pharisees put religious burdens on folk yet don't lift a finger to help. (v. 4)
- Pharisees do everything for public show, not for God. (v. 5)
- Pharisees love to be honored at civic or religious events. (v. 6)
- Pharisees love to be recognized in public as religious teachers. (v. 7)
- Pharisees exalt themselves, and they will be humbled. (v. 12)
- Pharisees reject God's kingdom and close its door to others. (v. 13)
- Pharisees work hard to gain converts, who become even worse bigots. (v. 15)
- Pharisees make oaths but look for ways to avoid keeping them. (vv. 16–18)
- Pharisees give tithes but neglect justice, mercy, and faithfulness. (v. 23)
- Pharisees focus on religious minutiae and miss the main point. (v. 24)
- Pharisees appear upright and clean but inside are full of moral filth. (v. 25)
- Pharisees claim to love Israel's prophets, but their sort killed the prophets. (vv. 29–32)
- Pharisees will reject God's coming prophets and kill them, too. (v. 34)

Three terms stand out through repetition:

1. Jesus uses the word woe seven times.

By using the term *woe* against them, Jesus adopts the traditional prophetic term used by Isaiah and Jeremiah in their warning and mourning over coming judgment. Most of Israel thought the Pharisees worthy of a "wow"—but Jesus declares woe! He does this seven times—seven being the Hebraic number for completeness. Was there no room left for repentance, or was Jesus saying they had filled up to the full the measure of God's indignation against their self-righteous religion?

2. Jesus labels them as "hypocrites" seven times.

They are not what they appear—the outside is not as the inside. They are actors playing a charade. Their profession is insincere, and they are frauds. Again the sevenfold repetition of this term underscores that they represent hypocrisy fully!

3. They are described as "blind" five times.

Though they believe they have found the way to God, they cannot see. They have not recognized God's coming. They are lost and are leading others astray.

As if all this were not enough, Jesus also says that these men who think they are destined for heaven are actually "son[s] of hell" (v. 15); they who think they are so wise and learned are "fools" (v. 17); they who think they are models of purity are "whitewashed tombs … full of … uncleanness" (v. 27 ESV); they who think they are sons of Abraham are "descendants of those who murdered" (v. 31); they who think they are law keepers are lawbreakers like "serpents" in Eden (v. 33 ESV).

If Jesus could say anything harsher or more insulting, it is hard to imagine what! Let us be clear again—these were the most "religious," most "respected," and believed themselves the most "righteous" of any group in Israel. And yet they incur the greatest assault on their religion. Being religious is not being righteous. Not all that glitters is gold. Not all that prays, worships, and tithes is holy. At times it may be quite the contrary.

That is why Jesus was so hard on the Pharisees. It was precisely because they weren't far from the truth, studying and teaching the Law of Moses, that they needed to be so severely challenged. Jesus gave the Sadducees far less of a verbal assault. But the Pharisees were nearer the truth, close enough to sound plausible and biblical, and so more able to lead people astray. Jesus was harshest with them because they were the closest to the truth and yet missed it for themselves and for others.

HOLY BY CONTRAST

The contrasts between the Pharisees' version of holiness and Jesus' make for salutary reading:

- The Pharisees' holiness made much of rules—Jesus' holiness made much of God.
- The Pharisees' holiness made much of themselves— Jesus' holiness made much of others.
- The Pharisees' holiness made much of externals, like washing hands—Jesus' holiness made much of internals, like washing the heart.
- The Pharisees' holiness kept company with the

scrupulously clean—Jesus' holiness kept company with the notoriously wicked.

- The Pharisees' holiness focused on oral interpretation of the law—Jesus' holiness focused on loving God and neighbor, which summed up the law.
- The Pharisees' holiness was exclusive—Jesus' holiness was inclusive.
- The Pharisees' holiness viewed God primarily as lawgiver—Jesus' holiness depicted God primarily as love giver.
- The Pharisees' holiness was inauthentic, a false-faced hypocrisy—Jesus' holiness was authentic through and through.
- The Pharisees' holiness focused on form—Jesus' holiness focused on substance.
- The Pharisees' holiness was the result of supposed merit—Jesus' holiness was a gift of mercy.
- The Pharisees' holiness caused them to reject the Holy One of Israel—Jesus' holiness caused him to reject the false shepherds and so-called holy ones of Israel.
- The Pharisees' holiness was quick to judge whatever differed from it—Jesus' holiness sought to forgive.
- The Pharisees' holiness led them to be murderers—Jesus' holiness led him to martyrdom.

WHY WAS THE RELIGION OF THE PHARISEES HARMFUL, NOT HOLY?

The pharisaical approach to holiness leads to disastrous

consequences: perfectionism, legalism, judgmentalism, privatism, and self-deception.[17]

1. Pharisaism is marked by perfectionism.

Driven by the command "be holy as I am holy," the Pharisees left little room for grace, mercy, and faith. One of the most repeated criticisms of Christ against Pharisaism was that it "lacked mercy"—it took no prisoners, was mean, hard, cold, and callous. The religion of the Pharisees was all about performance, attaining the standard of perfection in every area of their lives.

Living as those driven by such standard setting leads to pride in our perceived achievements, or, if we are more truly self-aware, to a crushing sense of guilt and the constant fear of failure. If we live our lives by this kind of holiness measure, when we fail to measure up, we will either give up or, worse, break down. We will also project that standard onto others around us and impart that spirit of condemnation to them. Our homes will become places of tension, pedantic scrutiny, lack of peace, and little laughter. John Oswalt said,

> To measure our acceptance by God on the basis
> of absolutely perfect performance of holiness, is
> to condemn ourselves to failure. God is the only
> one whose performance is absolutely holy.[18]

2. Pharisaism is marked by legalism.

The measure of holiness as loving God and loving our neighbor as ourselves is intangible. And so the pharisaic spirit looks for clearly defined criteria by which to assess and measure performance—not drinking, not smoking, not associating with certain "types," giving a certain percentage of income, dressing in a certain way, not going to certain places, behaving in particular ways on particular days.

Jesus' holiness is a matter of the heart—loving God and entering into closer communion with him—whereas pharisaical holiness is defined by a list of dos and don'ts, preferring rules over relationship with God.

For the Pharisees, religion was all about the Torah, temple, washings, set hours of prayer, fasting, and dissociation from the unclean. Their interests and devotions were elsewhere from God himself. God was almost never spoken of on their lips and was far from their hearts. Yahweh was not their burning passion; religiosity was.

This throws the spotlight on a great test of all our Christian efforts. What's the main word spoken? What is the primary subject—what am I most consciously aiming for? If that is not clearly, obviously, unequivocally God, as revealed in Jesus, then we have followed a tributary into trouble. If an outsider, observing what we are and do, says that one of these features stands out in our religion—exclusion and separation, dressing plainly and rejecting modern society's advances, saying confession, receiving Mass, praying, having quiet times, evangelizing, speaking in tongues, siding with the poor, *or anything less than the person and work of Jesus Christ himself*—then we have probably gone wrong somewhere. We have probably gotten religious and veered toward the values of Pharisaism.

Not that all of these are wrong. Indeed, some are very right. But if these distinctively define our expression of religion, rather than a clear-for-all-to-see, blazing passion to love God and our neighbor, together with an individual dependence on Jesus day by day, then we are in trouble. The sad fact is, for many Christians, such secondary things are very much primary. They become the defining criteria of religion and true holiness. And if they do, that may well put us in the category of Pharisees, who made hand washing, tithing, and dissociation from sinners the hallmark of holiness. The rebuke of Jeremiah seems highly apt: "How can you say, 'We are wise, for we have the law of the LORD,' when actually the lying pen of the scribes has handled it falsely?" (Jer. 8:8).

3. Pharisaism is marked by judgmentalism.

Performance measurement brings judgment: First we apply the judgment to ourselves, commending ourselves or, more often than not, condemning ourselves; then we apply the judgment to others, whether they want it or not! When our religion is based on performance, the tendency is to impose the same legalistic standards of holiness on others. Whether they are intending to follow a standard of holiness or not, they come under our scrutiny; and when they fall short, we quickly judge them—in our hearts, if not verbally. The Pharisees were quick to impose their values of religious purity on Jesus and his disciples, and when the followers of Jesus didn't conform to the Pharisees' standards of behavior, they were immediately rebuked and challenged. Some may suggest that Jesus himself displayed the same kind of judgmentalism toward their expression of religion as they did to his—indeed, some did think him too severe (Luke 19:27). But as a friend of mine has said: Grace presents a hard face to legalism.

4. Pharisaism is marked by privatism.

True holiness means loving and living for God and the world. The great problem with the Pharisees was the great focus of the

Pharisees—themselves! Dietrich Bonhoeffer, writing from prison before his execution, said that the church is only the church when she exists for others. If we are constantly fixated on ourselves and our performance as holy people, rather than on the Lord Jesus, our religion becomes navel gazing—all about me, not you, and not even about God!

A study of every statement by the Pharisees in the New Testament finds virtually no reference to God whatsoever! It's all me, me, me—how I am doing, how I am feeling, how I am ascending, how I am battling. Now, scripturally, God does call us to be self-aware, to bring our lives under his gaze (2 Cor. 13:5), but a legalistic and introspective pharisaic pursuit of holiness leads to neurosis, self-obsession, and even despair. One has only to consider Martin Luther before his revelation from Romans on justification by faith—fasting incessantly, confessing imaginary sins repeatedly, whipping himself till the blood flowed to punish out the evil—to see the psychological disaster brought on by such a false pursuit of holiness.

5. Pharisaism is marked by self-deception.

Having set their standards and gone after them, the Pharisees were quick to condemn others and commend themselves. They actually believed they were getting somewhere with God, yet all the while they were heading in the direction of hell. All that religion did not make them righteous. All that effort actually increased their sinfulness rather than bringing holiness. They were deceived—religious, passionate, concerned with holiness, but deceived. And so the very ones who believed themselves to be holy rejected the true holiness personified in Jesus Christ, God come in the flesh, and sought to annihilate it from their world. They worked religiously to have the Holy One of God arrested, tried, condemned, and crucified.

The Pharisees had no self-awareness. If they had, they would have cried out, "Woe is me, for God requires me to be as holy as he is—but I am a sinner, I fall short of his commands, I can never be holy as he is; all I can do is limp in the direction of his decrees while throwing myself on his grace and begging for mercy!" But no, they had to go it alone and think they could manage alone.

The Pharisees commended themselves for their holy efforts and were condemned for their unholy efforts. I can't help wondering … if Jesus were to come today, would some of us who think we are going hard after holiness actually reject him because he isn't holy in our way? I am sure that when Jesus returns, there will be many who have lived religious lives, have claimed to be pursuing righteousness and holiness, and yet have done it all for themselves, by themselves—and so Jesus will have to say, "I never knew you. Away from me" (Matt. 7:23). *Kyrie eleison.*

It has been rightly said, "Our holiness is never the cause of God's love for us,"[19] and here lies the root of every Pharisaic blunder. Their pursuit of holiness was an attempt to impress others, and no doubt to impress God as well—perhaps to merit both credit and affection. They failed to see that God's love was always unconditional, a given. Our holiness is never a factor in God's love for us—all our efforts cannot increase his love one iota. The call to holiness is the call from love to love; our pursuit of holiness is the straight highway of response of our love for the Beloved.

Chapter 6

Without Blame

> God condemned sin in Christ so that holiness
> might appear in us.[1]

I awoke to a white world. Pulling back my curtains, everything was coated in a fresh, thick fall of snow. All the usual imperfections, rubbish, dirt, and detritus of a city were covered—everything seemed pure, pristine, and perfect. The prophet Isaiah once promised: "Though your sins are like scarlet, they shall be as white as snow" (1:18). There is a profound longing in the heart of man—and, as we have seen, in the heart of God—to declare over us that our sins are covered and we are "white as snow." We have a name for that declaration, that removal of sin, which establishes for us a pure standing before God. It is justification.

LONGING TO BE JUSTIFIED

There was only one man who lived a perfect life, who conformed to God's command to "be holy as I am holy," and that was the Son of

God born of human flesh, Jesus Christ. While many refuse to recognize God and seek to remove themselves from the guilt of falling from God's character and order, many others are sufficiently honest with God and with themselves to admit they have failed. They can't keep their own New Year's resolution, let alone God's moral law. For these people, a very real sense of condemnation, guilt, and fear may follow.

Humanity's religious impulse—that dedicated commitment to the world religions with their competing and contradictory rules and rituals—is an attempt to remove the guilt experienced before God and awake to a world where sins are as white as snow. All sincere acts of religious devotion, pilgrimages to sacred shrines, sacrifices and offerings to idols, incense and intercessions spring from this attempt to justify oneself to God and to be found just, righteous, holy, accepted by God. But, with Lady Macbeth, they find

> all the perfumes of Arabia will not sweeten this
> little hand.[2]

Many have suggested that all religions are essentially the same and only superficially different. The prophet Isaiah and the apostle Paul would certainly disagree (Isa. 46; Rom. 1:21–23)! Yes, there are clear points of contact: They share a longing for purity, holy texts, holy people, holy places, holy rites, pursuit of the holy divine. However, as Ravi Zacharias often notes, the religions are, in fact, superficially the same and fundamentally different. That is most clearly true for Judeo-Christianity when compared to the rest. The essence of religion may be condensed down to this: First sanctify yourself, and then you may be justified before God. Christianity is radically different because it declares, *first God justifies us, and then he works with us toward sanctification.*

Analogously, we might think in terms of an exam. Most religions demand we work hard to pass the exam so God can accept us. Christianity claims God gives all who come to him a pass mark immediately and then tutors us on the exam questions.

THE ESSENCE OF JUSTIFICATION

> *Who shall bring any charge against God's elect? (Rom. 8:33 ESV)*

Justification is a theme that underpins all God's dealings with us. The English term derives from the Latin *justificare,* meaning "to show as just, innocent, and pure." It translates the Hebrew word group around *tsedeq,* meaning "righteousness, justice, right behavior, right standing." In Greek, the word group surrounding justification translates the word *dikaioo,* the root of which refers to punishment. Ancient Greek warriors used the word as a battle cry—"Justice! (Here comes punishment!)," but later it was used to define the core value of the state and applied to the model citizen.

In the New Testament, the word carries a judicial sense of being acquitted. All these words and phrases reflect its meaning: declared innocent, righteous, without blame, vindicated, pardoned, in the clear.

Now, to justify means to declare innocent, and because the sinner patently is not innocent, justification involves the moral imputation of innocence. This is not an empty declaration, a way of stating something untrue. No, justification declares righteousness on those who have been declared innocent by the presiding judge. This initial legal *imputation* is done in a moment; it is then followed up by an ongoing *impartation* of a righteousness in our characters, formed by the Holy Spirit as we comply with him and he transforms us into the likeness of Christ. Again, it is as if we are conferred the degree of Doctor of Holiness, and then we get down to studying to become what we have been declared.

This imputation has a double aspect, negative and positive. Negatively, our sin is no longer counted against us. Positively, Christ's righteousness is credited to our benefit. Paul drew on the psalmist to understand righteousness: "Blessed are they whose transgressions are forgiven, whose sins are covered" (Rom. 4:7); "Blessed is the man whose sin the LORD does not count against him" (Ps. 32:2).

Justification is the counterpart to unrighteousness—it is righteousness, holiness, right standing without guilt before God. Some time ago, because of the foolishness of a newspaper's article, a group of Premier League footballers walked free from court. The article was said to have possibly prejudiced the jury, and the trial was halted. Though the men walked free because of a legal technicality, they were not acquitted—a cloud still remains! The people, the police, and the judge will never consider those individuals innocent! That is *not* how we are to understand the biblical doctrine of justification. In biblical justification, we are not simply treated as though we are innocent— we are made innocent! We are both acquitted of guilt and fitted with righteousness (Rom. 3:21–22). Justification is pardoning absolutely. The sinner's slate is wiped totally clean.

In Scripture, justification is always passive; it is something we receive, not achieve. It comes from outside us, not within. No one ever justifies himself or herself: "But you were washed, you were sanctified, you were justified [you didn't do it yourself] in the name of the Lord Jesus Christ and by the Spirit of our God" (1 Cor. 6:11). Paul declared that, from all eternity, God "chose us in him … to be holy [sanctified] and blameless [justified] in his sight" (Eph. 1:4).

Justified and sanctified … you cannot have one without the other. Justification comes in a moment, maybe of crisis, infusing us with holiness and declaring us to be without blame. Sanctification always follows justification; the seeds of sanctification are sown in and with justification as we journey without fault into Christlikeness. Justification, righteousness, and sanctification are all closely interconnected. Justified, we are *without blame;* sanctified, we are becoming *without fault.*

GOD ALONE IS THE ONE WHO JUSTIFIES

> *God … justifies the wicked.… It is God who justifies.*
> *(Rom. 4:5; 8:33)*

We don't justify ourselves. We can't justify ourselves. In this context, all our righteousness is like filthy rags (Isa. 64:6; Zech. 3:3). We are judged against God's standard of righteousness and holiness; as sinners, we have fallen short of that absolute perfect standard. Our sin has violated God's standard, and God's justice must be meted out against sin. God's wrath must be satisfied by punishment. So it must be God who justifies us and satisfies himself. God is the active party here; he initiates and orchestrates our justification. The standard he sets for us is the standard he meets in us. That which God requires is that which

God provides. The wedding invitation comes with the gift of wedding clothes.

God says repeatedly in the Levitical law, "I am the LORD, who makes you holy" (Lev. 22:32). Having laid down rules defining holiness, God then says he is the one who makes his people holy. How? By providing alongside the legal system a sacrificial system to cover sin. The writer to the Hebrews speaks of Jesus as the one "who sanctifies" and his followers as "those who are sanctified" (Heb. 2:11 ESV).

We see God doing this in his dealings with all types—prophet, priest, and king. For Isaiah, who bewailed his sins as he beheld God, the word from the seraphim was, "Your guilt is taken away, and your sin atoned for" (Isa. 6:7 ESV). The high priest Joshua, finding himself standing before God in the filthy rags of sin, heard God declare, "Behold, I have taken your iniquity away from you, and I will clothe you with pure vestments" (Zech. 3:4 ESV). And when King David, confronted by Nathan for his adulterous sin with Bathsheba and the murder of Uriah, cries out to God, "I have sinned" immediately God's response comes through the prophet: "The LORD has taken away your sin" (2 Sam. 12:13).

In each case, we see a righteous standing established, sin's judgment passed, and justification imputed—all at God's initiative. The human desire for justification before God is never as strong as God's desire for the justification of humanity.

GOD'S GRACE IS THE BASIS FOR JUSTIFICATION

All have sinned and fall short of the glory of God,
and are justified freely by his grace. (Rom. 3:23–24)

This concept of justification as grace gift was very dear to Paul, no doubt because he had previously tried so hard and unsuccessfully to go it alone via the route of pharisaical Judaism. In Romans 5:15–17 he spoke five times of justification as a "free gift" that we have received from the "abundance of grace" (ESV). Justification comes *gratis;* it costs us nothing. It is freely ours, all of grace. It has to be free because we could not afford it—its worth is priceless. With nothing to pay, we come empty-handed. As the hymn puts it,

> Nothing in my hand I bring,
> Simply to Thy cross I cling.[3]

Only the sinless sacrifice of the Son could purchase redemption. God is a giving God. Most religions in their conceptions of God think we come to him with a gift; but we come with empty hands. We are the beneficiaries of the benevolent God.

Some object to grace through a sense of pride. They don't want a free handout; they want to make it on their own. Rather than receive the free handout of grace, many seek to justify themselves and make themselves righteous on the basis of their efforts. But that is like climbing the north face of the Eiger with your arms handcuffed behind your back. Such pride goes before a fall.

Good works are futile in attaining justification. While true faith produces good works (James 2:14) and while God has saved us in order to do good works (Eph. 2:10), nevertheless "by works of the law no human being will be justified in [God's] sight" (Rom. 3:20 ESV). Paul said that our great role model of faith is Abraham, who was not justified by works but by faith (Rom. 4:2–3). Even if the scales were to lean in favor of my right actions over my sinful ones, God does not judge on the basis of percentages but rather on the basis of perfection. No amount of human religious and moral effort can satisfy the divine requirement of purity.

ALL SINNERS ARE WITHIN THE SCOPE OF JUSTIFICATION

> *God ... will justify the circumcised by faith and the uncircumcised through that same faith. (Rom. 3:30)*

The ancient Jews divided the world into two categories—them and us, circumcised and uncircumcised, Jew and Gentile, clean and unclean. But now, said Paul, God makes no distinction—all, Jew and Greek, sinner and seeker, are the same. They have all fallen short of God's standard, the glorious perfection of God (Rom. 3:23). There are not different classes and certainly not different pathways to God. There are no two ways about it. All people *can only be* justified by one means. And all people *may be* justified by that one means. No one is outside the reach of grace. No sinner, no sin, is so vile that it cannot be covered. The hand of justification always trumps that of condemnation.

JESUS' BLOOD IS THE GROUND OF JUSTIFICATION

> *Justified ... through the redemption that came by Christ Jesus. God presented him as a sacrifice of atonement, through faith in his blood. (Rom. 3:24–25)*

By faith in Christ, we are united with him in his death and life, and when God sees us, he sees not our sin but our clothing by the righteousness of his Son. But this clothing came at great cost. As J. Rodman Williams said, it is not a casual matter to declare man righteous:

> Justification is grounded in the costly deed of redemption, the bloody death of the sinless Jesus.[4]

God cannot simply offer us justification without first the satisfaction of his righteous judgment against sin. To negate his righteousness would be to render him unrighteous. Divine judgment in punishment must be spent.

Paul spoke of propitiation. In classical Greek, the term he used (*hilasterion*) meant to satisfy or avenge the wrath of the gods. Many have tried to tone this down for the biblical sense, not wanting to think of God as getting angry at sin and sinners. (The story goes that one young lad, when asked the difference between the Old Testament and the New, said that in the New Testament God became a Christian.) Consequently, some render Paul's word as *expiation,* meaning that sin is covered or wiped away. That, of course, is true, but it is not the whole truth. Sin can be removed only when the sin is judged, when God's righteous wrath is satisfied. How can this happen? One thing's for sure: We can't pull it off.

Mysteriously, miraculously, and mercifully, God accomplished this by permitting his sinless Son (for only God could meet such an immense debt) to become human (for only a human should pay for sin). And God laid on Christ the iniquity of us all (Isa. 53:6).

Jesus, who knew no sin, became sin for us (2 Cor. 5:21). Violently he died, a sacrifice, a substitute, a satisfaction. When the Father by the Spirit raised him to life, it's as though he said, "Debt paid; Christ's death is sufficient; I am satisfied." Adolf Köberle neatly defined justification as

> pardon for sin and acceptance by God on the basis of Jesus' shed blood.[5]

Hebrews 10:10 says, "We have been sanctified through the offering of the body of Jesus Christ once for all" (ESV). Justification may cost us nothing, but it does cost, and God himself paid. God's own beloved Son willingly laid down his life on the altar of Golgotha.

TRUSTING FAITH IS THE CONDUIT OF JUSTIFICATION

> *[God is] just and the one who justifies those who have faith in Jesus. (Rom. 3:26)*

What is faith? It is not a blind, unquestioning mystical leap. It is a reasoned response to the historical work of Christ in his life, death, and resurrection. Faith is focused at the cross, coming from a personal trust in the effects and benefits of that work. Justification by faith alone is the central doctrine that separated Protestants from Catholics at the Reformation. Catholics had whittled away the biblical basis of salvation and replaced it with rules and regulations and responsibilities that had to be met through the effort of the individual before justification could be known. (And money given to the church or martyrdom fighting in a crusade might cause God to look favorably on you too.) Protestants protested. Justification is by grace alone, through faith alone, in Christ alone.

Martin Luther was the great prophet of the Reformation. He was an Augustinian monk who lived at the close of the medieval period in a monastery in Erfurt, Germany, but Augustinianism had fallen a long way from its namesake's doctrines. Riddled with guilt and condemnation, Luther sought ferociously to exorcise himself of all darkness and justify himself before God, others, and himself. He fasted every third day, repeatedly whipped himself, and went weekly to confession—until his superiors worried about the state of his mind! On visiting Rome, he climbed the steps of the Scala Santa on bloodied knees … as if his blood would impress God.

Then, one day while he was reading Romans, his heart and mind were opened to the biblical truth that "the righteous will live by faith" (Rom. 1:17). Faith, not works; God's sacrifice, not his own; gift, not grit; Christ, not him. From that moment on, Luther taught and fought unceasingly for this truth and with it restored the church to her source of life.

PEACE IS THE EXPERIENCE OF JUSTIFICATION

Since we have been justified through faith, we have peace with God through our Lord Jesus Christ, through whom we have gained access by faith into this grace in which we now stand. And we rejoice in the hope of the glory of God. (Rom. 5:1–2)

What great peace flooded Luther's mind with the revelation that his justification relied on faith and not effort! He now understood four immediate and direct benefits of justification, as identified by Paul:

1. peace
2. access to God's grace
3. rejoicing
4. hope

Surely these are what all religious longing is directed toward; it's just that religious effort divorced from faith and grace will never deliver them. Justification by works can lead to pride at one's own imagined achievements—though, more realistically, it leads to anxiety as we realize that our efforts have brought God no nearer.

The Devil will tell you that you can justify yourself on your own, only to fill you with guilt and condemnation when you fail to show evidence of this. But there is now no condemnation for those who are in Christ Jesus, in whom the righteous requirement of the law is fulfilled through being justified (Rom. 8:1–3).

BE AWARE OF THE BATTLE

This doctrine of justification—by grace alone, through faith alone, in Christ alone—is the key to understanding the nature of God, the work of Christ, and the uniqueness of Christianity. Calvin called it "the principal ground upon which religion must be supported."[6] It is the greatest message the world has ever heard—declared right, put right, righteous as a free gift that cost God his only Son, through whom we may be washed, sanctified, justified.

Perhaps we shouldn't be surprised, then, that this doctrine more than most has been the subject of vicious spiritual warfare. Justification as God's saving economy to sanctify us positionally and fit us for heaven eternally disgusts our satanic Enemy, and he constantly undermines it. He may tell us we are so sinful we'll never receive it; or alternatively, we aren't too bad and don't need it; or we may earn it ourselves by religion, by self-sanctification. The Devil has always been the slave master who would have us make religious bricks without straw.

The church has constantly undermined, challenged, and withheld this great and glorious gift from the world and from herself. Paul wrote this detailed treatment of justification to inform the church how central it is to the gospel and how essential it is to the Christian understanding of our life and identity. This battle to play down justification was seen in the church of the Galatians, whom Paul rebuked as being deceived as by witchcraft and called back to a gospel of justification by faith. The same battle raged in the fourth-century church, as we have already seen, when the English bishop Pelagius argued that we are able to take steps toward our own sanctification by our own efforts. The heresy was aggressively countered by Augustine, who demonstrated that justification was purely a gift of grace to the one who has faith, and Pelagianism was rightly declared a heresy at the Council of Carthage in 418. Luther simply followed where Paul and Augustine had first trod.

And he wasn't to be the last. In the nineteenth century, the rise of liberal theology argued for the ability of human beings to create in and of themselves conditions for the kingdom of heaven on earth. Evangelicalism and Pentecostalism both saw justification by faith as central, and this brought a much-needed biblical balance. Adolf Köberle, in his work *The Quest for Holiness,* bemoaned the tragedy that "the church did not guard the message as carefully as she should have," resulting in a "momentous dissolution and disintegration of the truth."[7]

We'll let Martin Luther have the last word: "I have preached justification by faith so often, and I feel sometimes that you are so slow to receive it, that I could almost take the Bible and bang it about your heads."[8]

Chapter 7
Without Fault

We have seen that the religious impulse in humankind is often driven by a longing for the justification that only God can give. Whereas other religions believe justification *proceeds* from personal sanctification, the distinctive in Christianity is to see that justification *precedes* personal sanctification. Our sins cannot be covered by our good works, which can never make us righteous. Only God can do that, and he does do that for those who look to his Son.

IF YOU ARE JUSTIFIED, YOU WILL BE SANCTIFIED

The Bible shows that justification will lead to sanctification. God loves us the way we are at justification, but he doesn't leave us there. Having justified us, he wants to sanctify us. The great Victorian Anglican bishop J. C. Ryle once wrote:

> Tell me not of your justification, unless you have also some marks of sanctification. Boast not of

Christ's work for you, unless you can show us the Spirit's work in you.[1]

The prophetic Reformer Martin Luther thundered:

> There is no justification without sanctification, no forgiveness without renewal of life, no real faith from which the fruits of new obedience do not grow.

When justification is imputed to the believer, the seed of sanctification is sown.

I'll never forget my oldest son Joel's eighth birthday. His younger brother Nat came into my room and said in surprise, "He isn't eight—he hasn't grown any taller!" In Nat's mind, the change of age that day should have been instantly recognizable by gain in height. Of course, we know that physical growth is more gradual, and, whether or not we can expect physical growth as we age over the years, we are certainly to expect spiritual growth. That growth is growth into the likeness of God, toward whom we move.

New birth should be followed up with growth. Birth is instant, while growth is a lifetime process—but, unless the child is sick, growth is the inevitable fruit of birth. Even as a seed has within it the power of germination and plant growth, so newborn believers have inherent within them that which brings growth. Jonathan Edwards said that the desire for sanctification is an innate impulse in the regenerate:

> 'Tis as much the nature of one that is spiritually new born, to thirst after growth in holiness, as 'tis

the nature of a newborn babe, to thirst after the mother's breast.[2]

We are *made* holy by virtue of the incoming of the Holy Spirit when we are reborn, and we *become* holy by virtue of the exercise and outworking of the Holy Spirit in us as we grow.

SO WHAT'S THE DIFFERENCE?

Contrasting justification with sanctification, New Testament scholar S. E. Porter said,

> Sanctification is not a synonymous term but a development, actualisation or consequence of justification in the believer's life.[3]

So we can observe the following life-changing facts:[4]

- Justification is to be without blame; sanctification is to be without fault.
- Justification is the foundation for sanctification; sanctification is never the foundation for justification.
- Justification is the reckoning of someone as righteous in Christ; sanctification is the making of someone righteous in themselves.
- Justification is a righteousness not of one's own—it is imputed; sanctification is a righteousness by partnering with God's Spirit—it is imparted.

- In justification, works have no place—it is all of faith and grace; in sanctification, works are crucial—good works joining grace and faith.
- Justification admits no growth or increase—one cannot be more or less justified; sanctification is something we grow in.
- Justification is a one-off gift that cannot be given or taken back; sanctification is a progressive state that we can also regress in.
- Justification is monergistic—a work solely of God in us; sanctification is synergistic—a partnership between us and the Spirit.

A HOLY WORK

The rather churchy term *sanctification,* from the Latin words *sanctus* (holy) and *facere* (to work), corresponds with the Old Testament Hebrew word *qadosh*. The root meaning is "to cut" and refers to being separate for God. The same is true of the New Testament word *hagiasmos,* from the word group relating to holiness or separation.

That is what the word means at root, but how has it been defined and understood in church reflection?

The seventeenth-century English Puritan John Owen spoke of it as

a virtue, a power, a principle of the spiritual life and grace, wrought, created, infused into our souls, antecedent to and the next cause of true acts of holiness.[5]

The eighteenth-century American scholar and revivalist Jonathan Edwards said:

> Sanctification is the beauty of the Holy Spirit becoming the perfecting beauty of our humanity too, which is created to be indwelt by the Holy Spirit. The Holy Spirit, as Divine Love, activates our Holy Affections of love to God, without which we are incomplete.[6]

The nineteenth-century Baptist theologian A. H. Strong said:

> Sanctification is that continuous operation of the Holy Spirit, by which the holy disposition imparted at regeneration is maintained and strengthened.[7]

In a similar tradition, twentieth-century Louis Berkhof wrote of

> that gracious and continual operation of the Holy Spirit, by which he delivers the justified sinner from the pollution of sin, renews his whole nature in the image of God, and enables him to perform good works.[8]

Modern-day theologian Millard Erickson defines sanctification in relation to Christ:

> the Spirit at work in the believer, bringing about the likeness to Christ.[9]

As does Sinclair Ferguson:

> The Holy Spirit works in regeneration ... to unite
> us to Christ.... The goal of his activity is transfor-
> mation into the likeness of Christ.[10]

These fairly standard definitions point to something that is ascribed to the believer as both the initial status conferred on us (justification) and a process that continues to be wrought in us (sanctification). They emphasize the driving activity of the Holy Spirit in the process and the likeness of Christ as the goal, with good works as both evidence and means of sanctification.

CRISIS AND PROCESS

So we see that God imputes positional sanctification (justification) to us in a moment, the instant one believes and receives. This initiates the Christian life but then leads to a practical sanctification process, whereby we as Christians, established righteous through Christ's righteousness imputed to us, then seek to become practically what we are positionally. Jürgen Moltmann emphasized that

> sanctification as a gift leads to sanctification as a
> charge.[11]

The great struggle of the Christian life is to become what we are, to allow the Holy Spirit to make us into Christ's image. To use the technical terms of grammar for a moment, the *indicative* of the believer receiving the Spirit must be wed to the *imperative* of the believer walking in the Spirit. Our new life as saints must lead to our new lifestyle as sanctified. Repeatedly in Scripture, we are labeled as saints (Rom. 1:7; 8:27; 16:2, 15; Eph. 1:1, 15, 18; 3:18; 6:18), but for Paul, holiness is both a present condition and an ongoing process.[12] Again, to speak grammatically, holiness is both a noun (what we are) and a verb (what we do). That is why Brian Doerksen is right to make us sing, "I choose to be holy."[13] This is a reference to the active part we play in the process after we have been justified.

Paul addressed his first letter to the Corinthians "to the church of God in Corinth … those sanctified in Christ Jesus called to be holy" (1:2). They were called to become practically what they were positionally. Though they had the Spirit in residence (3:16), these particular Christians were marked by deep carnality and a lack of spirituality, resulting in immaturity, immorality, and idolatry. Unsaintly saints!

The Ephesians are described positionally as saints (1:1), having been reconciled, redeemed, and adopted into God's family. They have received the Holy Spirit (1:13), but they are challenged not to grieve the Holy Spirit (4:30) through sins of body and soul—fleshly cravings and actions and a use of mind, emotion, and will, which have not been permeated by the Holy Spirit, who lives with the human spirit. In 2 Corinthians 5:17–19, Paul spoke of the church as new creations—reconciled to God—whose sins are not held against them (positional); however, shortly after, (7:1) he called them to "purify [them]selves from everything that contaminates" (practical). The writer to the Hebrews spoke of God who "by one sacrifice … has made perfect forever those who are being made holy" (10:14). Positionally "perfected"; practically "being made holy."

Let's take a look at five key facts about the process of sanctification.

1. Sanctification is essential.

> *Be holy; without holiness no one will see the Lord.*
> *(Heb. 12:14)*

> *It is God's will that you should be sanctified.... For*
> *God did not call us to be impure, but to live a holy*
> *life. Therefore, he who rejects this instruction does not*
> *reject man but God, who gives you his Holy Spirit.*
> *(1 Thess. 4:3, 7–8)*

Often we have the misconception that some special, elite group of Christians are called to holiness and manage to attain it. But holiness is not a special calling of the few whom we call "saints" and put on a pedestal of purity, as if the rest of us are not saints. In this we fail to comprehend that God never intended there to be a special category who attain a higher holiness than the rest. Holiness is the calling of all Christians. No one is exempt from this call. It is not the PhD of the Christian faith—it is elementary level, Christianity 101.

God went to hell and back to purchase our forgiveness and give us access to holiness. Not to pursue sanctification is to trample the blood of Jesus underfoot (Heb. 10:26–29)—it is to make a mockery of the misery and mercy of Calvary. It is to reject the work of the Holy Spirit, given to make us holy.

Holiness is essential because it fulfills God's will for us, it fulfills God's best for us, and it fulfills God's death for us. Our sanctification is not an end in itself—holiness fits us to be ministers to God (1 Peter 2:5) and to the world (2:9, 12). But no doubt the main reason God desires us to be holy is because he wants us close to him. Without holiness, we won't see God, and God wants us to see him. Being holy as he is holy means being with God and for God and receiving all we can from God.

2. Sanctification is for the whole person.

> *May ... the God of peace ... sanctify you through and through. May your whole spirit, soul and body be kept blameless at the coming of our Lord Jesus Christ.* (1 Thess. 5:23)

Holiness is not a social behavior code—the Pharisees treated it as such, and we saw what short shrift Jesus gave them. Holiness is to permeate every part of our being—it is not merely a set of external rules. Paul spoke of being sanctified "through and through"—thoroughly, not superficially. Paul spoke of the sanctification of spirit, soul, and body. In this context, spirit is the eternal self that was dead until Christ came and brought life to it. The soul is mind, intellect, and will. The body is, well, the body. Holiness must affect the totality of our being.

Note the order of sanctification—from inside out. Many have reduced holiness to external behavior, rules, dos and don'ts, thinking that by doing these with their body they will purify their soul and spirit. That's religion, and it doesn't work. The Pharisees were clean on the outside but whitewashed sepulchres full of death inside (Matt. 23:27).

After the Second World War, evangelical Christians emphasized holiness in externals like "no drinking, no smoking, no dancing." The Amish or Mennonites would emphasize externals like dressing plainly and not using modern technology. Plymouth Brethren would insist that men not wear ties and women not cut their hair. Believers were to be separate. They would not be expected to go into business with unbelievers or even live in a house that was attached to non-Brethren.

But these are externals. At best, they are good for the body, but such laws are powerless to change the soul and spirit—without which most seem rather irrelevant. The externally pious but internally impure is a hypocrite—as Jesus said, "First clean the inside of the cup and dish, and then the outside also will be clean" (Matt. 23:26). God has always looked on the heart, not the outward appearance (1 Sam. 16:7). Holiness can never be from outside in, always inside out. Thorough sanctification can never be a veneer of externals. God calls us to purify our spirits first and then our souls and bodies.

3. Sanctification is progressive.

> *Let us purify ourselves from everything that contaminates body and spirit, perfecting holiness out of reverence for God. (2 Cor. 7:1)*

We are to be constantly making progress in our Christian life— Scripture is very harsh on those it calls backsliders, who regress in holiness (see the next section). The perfecting of holiness speaks of the Christian goal as attaining to the perfect state of holiness. Now, grammatically, "perfecting holiness" is a present participle, denoting both continuous and habitual cleansing. *Robertson's Word Pictures of the New Testament* says this word refers to an

> aggressive and progressive … holiness, not a sudden attainment of complete holiness, but a continuous process.[14]

Paul could have worded this in such a way as to make this a fully realizable event now, but he didn't, and this further suggests that a daily process is what he had in mind.

New Testament scholar Murray Harris concurred:

> A process of sanctification … is involved … not the acquisition of perfect holiness. The same person who affirmed that he had "not yet reached perfection" and that his calling was perpetually to "press forward" (Phil. 3:12–14) would hardly envisage a permanent arrival at holiness in this present age. From 1 Thess. 3:13 it is clear that believers are "unblameable in holiness" or "faultlessly pure" … only at the second advent.[15]

Sanctification as both process and progress finds its consummation in eternity. Paul was sure that "he who began a good work in you will carry it on to completion until the day of Christ Jesus"

(Phil. 1:6). Despite appearances to the contrary, the promise is in place that one day, work in progress will be finished. The apostle John combined this present-day practical process with the eternal promise: "When he appears, we shall be like him, for we shall see him as he is. Everyone who has this hope in him purifies himself, just as [Christ] is pure" (1 John 3:2–3). How do we purify ourselves? By resisting sin, obeying God's commands, abiding in his love, walking in his Spirit. We do this in expectation that, when we finally see him, we will be fully conformed into his likeness.

4. Sanctification may be regressive.

While sanctification can and should be a process of progress, becoming ever nearer to and more like Christ, the reality is that many make little or no progress. Regrettably, some even go backward. After years of seeking God and growing into his likeness, the hard knocks of life, the temptations of the world, the afflictions of the Enemy, the rising of old roots of sin not removed can cause the believer to pull back from pursuing holiness, even willfully embracing sinfulness. So, while some progress in holiness, others tragically regress to worldliness.

The parable of the sower makes this very plain when Jesus tells us that, of the three types who receive the word of God (the gospel), two of the three fail to follow through in their discipleship, knocked back either by tribulation and persecution in life or by the cares of this world and the deceitfulness of riches (Mark 4:16–19). We all know of people who were once going hard after God but who stepped back or were knocked back and now either don't attend church or certainly have lost their zeal for the things of God. We have all heard of ministers and church members who once ran a good race but fell away through immorality. Paul, full of sadness, wrote to the Galatians, who had been "running a good race" until something cut in on them and prevented them from running (5:7).

Scripture all too often shows us this pattern of what is termed "spiritual backsliding." Too many of the leaders of Israel and Judah who once followed God faithfully fell away into sin. Gideon, so powerfully used of God in defeating the Midianites, slid back through pride and idolatry (Judg. 8). Saul, anointed by God as a prophet and king, became rebellious, disobedient to God's commands, and ultimately full of demonic rage against God's chosen anointed, David (1 Sam. 15:26–28). David—who is described in the New Testament as a man after God's own heart, who achieved great feats trusting in God, who heard from God and prophesied about the Messiah and wrote psalms that became Scripture—fell into gross immorality, taking another man's wife and then murdering the husband in an attempt to cover up his sin (2 Sam. 11). David's son Solomon, filled with God's wisdom, writer of Scripture's Ecclesiastes and much of Proverbs, builder of the great temple in Jerusalem, was drawn away into idolatry through his pagan wives (1 Kings 11). The whole history of Israel can be seen through the motif of this cycle of faithfulness (bringing blessing), backsliding (bringing judgment, invasion, or exile), and return to God (bringing restoration).

Not surprisingly, the New Testament addresses itself to backsliding. Jesus warned about salt losing its saltiness (Matt. 5:13). The letters to the Corinthians are addressed to a church community, filled with the Spirit, lacking no spiritual charism, and yet marked by sexual immorality, idolatry, divisions, and schisms, succumbing to culture rather than being sanctified by Christ. Jesus prophesied to the church at Ephesus that they had "forsaken [their] first love" (Rev. 2:4), having lost the initial passion for Christ and his work that they once had. The writer to the Hebrews warned the Christians not to sneak back to the synagogues to find safety from the suffering they were enduring. Paul reported that Demas, a fellow worker, had abandoned both him and Christ because he loved the world (2 Tim. 4:10). How tragic it is that, all too often, rather than advance into holiness, many return to the sin they were saved from, as a dog returns to its vomit (Prov. 26:11). In this context, we need something of the redoubtable spirit of former Prime Minister Margaret Thatcher, who defiantly stated, "This lady's not for turning."

But God is gracious. He waits, longing for the prodigals to return, and when they come to their senses, he runs to meet them, kissing, embracing, and restoring them (Luke 15). Jesus is the Good Shepherd who leaves the ninety-nine to go after the one, wooing, warning, seeking to bring that wandering sheep back into the fold. The Old Testament shows us God repeatedly sending the prophets to call his people back to himself—he never gives up on them but sends the word time and time again because he has compassion on them (2 Chron. 36:15). He is always trying to find ways of bringing the backsliders back to himself (Jer. 2:17–19; 3:22). And if they return, and if they repent, they are welcomed and restored. But they must repent and start again from that place of backsliding. C. S. Lewis wrote,

A wrong sum can be put right, but only by going back till you find the error and working it afresh from that point—never simply going on.[16]

If you are tempted to pull back from holy endeavor, know that he is able to keep you from falling and present you blameless before his glorious face (Jude 1:24). And what of those who don't repent? I believe they are still loved, still forgiven, still saved—but they lose their peace and joy in this life and their reward and crown in the next. Yet we are not to be those who shrink back (Heb. 10:39) but who believe and who press on toward Christ and Christlikeness.

5. Sanctification is active.

Some believe that holiness comes through a passivity, a letting go and a letting God. In this tradition is the highly influential spiritual writer Hannah Whitall Smith, who wrote of attaining

a way of holiness wherein the redeemed soul might live and walk in abiding peace, more than a conqueror.[17]

And how do we do this?

It is simply ceasing from all efforts of our own and trusting in the Lord to make us holy.[18]

She claimed a "sanctification by faith," a "second blessing" following justification by faith.[19]

But this notion of ceasing from all efforts seems to me to be entirely unbiblical. While the call to "not strive" is given by the psalmist in the context of worry, or indeed resisting God's Spirit, elsewhere striving is commended. J. C. Ryle rightly argued throughout his book *Holiness* that there are no gains without pains. Sanctification is painful—God disciplines us for our good so that we may share in his holiness (Heb. 12:10).

Whether it is a supposed endowment of the Spirit or an abandonment and surrender to Christ that we seek, there is a danger that we are in fact trying to avoid the crucible that shapes holy character. Perhaps those who seek entire sanctification as the result of a crisis experience can't face the sheer effort and personal cost involved in attaining holiness—the daily dying to sin, the crucifying of the flesh, the facing and overcoming of temptations. Yet, like Jesus, we are to learn obedience through the things we suffer (Heb. 5:8).

John Stott said that

> the search for Christian growth and fulfillment without acknowledging the cost of Christian discipleship, is still a major temptation today.[20]

He saw this most in charismatic and Pentecostal circles. Certainly the emphasis on receiving counseling, inner healing, or prayer ministry, where the recipient waits passively, eyes closed and hands open for the prayer to "do the stuff," can easily create a culture of passivity that refuses to take personal responsibility for sin. We should not keep looking to God to do what God calls *us* to do!

We don't have time here to explore these texts, but note the many responsibilities, the imperatives given to us where action is expected from us to move toward sanctification:

We are called to:

- train the soul—1 Timothy 4:7
- abide in Christ to bear fruit—John 15:1–17 (ESV)
- walk in the Spirit—Galatians 5:16 (ESV)
- imitate God—Ephesians 5:1 (ESV)
- walk in the light—Ephesians 5:8 (ESV)
- behold the Son—2 Corinthians 3:18 (ESV)
- live as sacrifices—Romans 12:1
- renew our minds—Romans 12:2
- submit to God—James 4:7
- resist the Devil—James 4:7
- wash hands and hearts—James 4:8
- throw off sin—Hebrews 12:1–4
- live to righteousness—Matthew 5—7; Romans 6:18
- press for perfection—Philippians 3:12 (verse 17: "imitate me")
- count ourselves dead—Romans 6:11
- put to death what belongs to the earthly nature—Colossians 3:5
- purify ourselves from contamination—2 Corinthians 7:1

Now, in all these we are not on our own. As many Reformed theologians are at pains to point out, just as we *begin* the Christian life by grace received through faith by the Spirit, so we are to *continue* through the Christian life toward sanctification by grace, through faith and the reception of the Spirit. But whereas in justification we were solely passive recipients, in sanctification we are active partners. Holiness is unobtainable without God's grace, but it is also unobtainable without our grit! Yes, grit. Obedience, dying to sin's appetite in the face of temptation.

So we must heed Karl Barth, who said that the man who thinks he can become sanctified on his own effort is "a fugitive of grace"[21]—only the rain and sun of God's grace grow the harvest of righteousness; nevertheless, those who leave it all to God are like the farmer who looked for a crop without plowing the field and planting the seeds.

SO IS SANCTIFICATION ATTAINABLE NOW?

Many have asked why, if God commands it, holiness would be unattainable. Would he command what we couldn't deliver? If God gives us the Holy Spirit to be holy, why shouldn't it be practically possible? While most Christians believe we will be perfected by God's grace only when we appear before him at death, or on Christ's return, others suggest it is a state the Christian can enter in this life. Certainly, as Professor Margaret Thrall said of the command to set about "perfecting holiness" in 2 Corinthians 7:1, "there must be some element of present fulfillment."[22]

Several evangelical traditions suggest an actual and total fulfillment in this life. We have already examined John Wesley's influential teaching on the experience of sinless perfection, which later Pentecostalism morphed from a baptism of holiness into a baptism of power (see chapter 4). The early-twentieth-century Keswick "higher life" tradition, with great churchmen like Andrew Murray and F. B. Meyer, also argued for a state of sinless perfection, coming not through effort but through passive surrender, "letting go and letting God." Others emphasized perfection coming through a constant recognition of one's being dead to sin, emphasizing Romans 6. Famous twentieth-century Bible teacher J. Sidlow Baxter claimed that

> entire sanctification in the sense of a major divine intervention in the already regenerated soul is not only soundly inferable from scripture, but amply attested by Christian experience.[23]

And again,

> Entire sanctification often or usually comes by way of a post-conversion crisis.… Entire sanctification must necessarily begin instantaneously as it begins precisely at the crisis point of utter hand-over to the divine possession.[24]

But many object to this (myself among them!), as we are unable to find one Scripture that directly supports entire perfection—not one biblical character (apart from Jesus) who is commended for perfection or described to suggest perfection. On the contrary, the weight of the New Testament epistles, written by various apostles to different churches at different times, is to exhort the church to ongoing personal sanctification. John Stott said that this view of "entire sanctification" is not something he has seen in his experience, nor is it "true to scripture."[25] C. H. Spurgeon famously kicked a man hard in the shins to make him lose his temper when he claimed he hadn't sinned for years! Paul at the start of his ministry almost boasted that he was the "apostle to the Gentiles" (Rom. 11:13). Later he described himself as the "least of the apostles" (1 Cor. 15:9), and approaching death, he said he was the worst of sinners (1 Tim. 1:15). Did he backslide over those years? Hardly. As he pressed on to know Christ (Phil. 3:8–12) he saw himself more clearly in the light of the glory and purity of Christ, and that proximity to divinity revealed his own sin more clearly.

Bishop J. C. Ryle once wrote:

> A deep sense of that struggle, and a vast amount of mental discomfort from it, are no proof that a man is not sanctified. Nay, rather, I believe they are healthy symptoms of our condition.... A true Christian is one who has not only peace of conscience, but war within. He may be known by his warfare as well as by his peace.[26]

As Thomas Cranmer wrote in Article 15 of the Thirty-Nine Articles, drawing on 1 John 1:8, "Although baptized, and born again in Christ, [we] offend in many things; and if we say we have no sin, we deceive ourselves, and truth is not in us."[27]

I am persuaded that sinless perfection is not a crisis experience after justification but rather the goal of sanctification, through a continual process throughout the believer's entire life.

Having said that, however, our mind-set will inevitably influence our action. If we believe pessimistically that we will always be defeated by sin, we will no doubt passively give in to it. If we believe optimistically that sinless perfection is a state we can enter one day, even today, through obedience to God and reliance on his Spirit, then we are more likely to live up to that. Daily we must awake and prayerfully choose, this day, to live free from sin, to walk fully in the Spirit. No Christian should ever be content with or resigned over sin in his or her life.

SO AIM HIGH

What can we say, then, with confidence about our sanctification?

Sanctification brings holiness, changing us into God's likeness. It makes positional righteousness personal, as that which is imputed to us at justification becomes a reality in our lives. Scripture speaks of sanctification as justification, transformation, and consummation: an accomplished event (1 Cor. 6:11), a present struggle (Heb. 10:14), and a future hope (1 Thess. 5:23).

Sanctification has a negative aspect—daily dying to the sins and stains of Adam's sinful programming of our flesh that cling so tightly (Heb. 12:1)—and a positive aspect—quickening the new nature in the likeness of Christ. It affects the whole of our being—body, soul, and spirit. It is a work performed in partnership between the Spirit of God and the action of the believer. It is aided by the disciplined life of prayer, service, worship, fasting, sacrifice, communion, study, obedience, and not being conformed to this world.

Sanctification is an internal work evidenced externally through personal Christlike character and good works to the benefit of others. It becomes a holy habit through the habitation of the Holy Spirit.

Sanctification is a journey, as we become in practice what we are called to be when we first believe. Entire sanctification, though only realized at the end of life or the end of history, must be the passionate aim and tenacious work of every believer.

Chapter 8
Jesus: The Holy One of God

P. T. Forsyth wrote over a century ago, and he is still worth quoting at length:

> We have seen in Christ a holiness the prophet did not know. It is not less solemn, it is not less sublime, but it is more sweet, it is more deep, it is more abiding. It is not a vision, but a presence and a power. We have seen through the smoke which filled the house. We have seen the *face* of Him that sat upon the throne. We have seen the Cross upon the altar. We have seen that the holiness of God is the holiness of love. There is no such awful gulf fixed between the King and the creature. We too are kings in Him. The word we hear is judgment indeed, and fear, but it is more. It is our judgment laid on the Holy. It is such mercy, pity, peace, and love. It is, indeed, infinite tenderness;

but it is soul tenderness, it is moral tenderness, it is atoning, redeeming tenderness. It is the tenderness of the Holy, which does not soothe but save. It is love which does not simply comfort, and it is holiness which does not simply doom. It is holy love, which judges, saves, forgives, cleanses the conscience, destroys the guilt, reorganises the race, and makes a new world from the ruins of the old.[1]

THE IMITATION OF HOLINESS PERSONIFIED

"Be holy as I am holy" is the divine invitation to divine imitation—arguably a theme that explains the whole biblical drama. This incredible beckoning of God to be like him expresses his longing for us to be with him, for without holiness no one will see the Lord (Heb. 12:14). The holiness God requires is the holiness God imparts through the sacrifice of his Son and our faith in that sacrifice.

We have seen that the positional holiness imputed to us in an instant must be followed up by practical holiness imparted over a lifetime of faithful discipleship. The good news is that Jesus is both the means of our positional holiness *and* the model for our practical holiness.

Chick Yuill wrote:

All too often our holiness teaching starts from the wrong place. Let us be clear that holiness does not begin at the point of surrender and crisis in the life of the believer.... It is too man-centred, too

self-orientated, too sin-centred. The place for it to
begin is with Jesus Christ and his perfect adequacy.[2]

On being confronted by the call to "be holy as I am holy," we
may well reply, "Yes, but what does 'holy' look like?" Jesus is our
supreme example. As God's own Son, he alone is truly holy as God
is holy. For us, holiness is Christlikeness. God is the perfection of
holiness—thrice holy (Rev. 4:8). Jesus said that if we have seen him
we have seen the Father (John 14:7–9). Jesus is thus the incarnation
of the perfection of holiness. As the perfect, holy Son of God, all that
Jesus did and said was holy. His whole act—being and speaking—
was holy. Nothing in his life deviated from the perfection of God.
N. T. Wright said that holiness is fashioning our lives "according to
that pattern of the perfect life, that of Christ."[3]

In recent years a popular movement has sprung up (echoing a similar movement from the 1890s) called "What Would Jesus Do?" People
wear badges and bands with a WWJD logo, reminding them to act in
any given situation according to the criterion of what Jesus would do
if he were in this kind of situation. In principle, this is training in holiness, an attempt to live, move, and have our being in Christ who lived,
moved, and had his being in holiness. True holiness is being conformed
into Christ's likeness, aided by the Spirit (2 Cor. 3:18). It is the basis
and goal of our salvation (Rom. 8:29). As Luther said, we're called to be
"little Christs." The Christian is called to the imitation of Christ—to
be holy as he is holy. The theologian G. C. Berkouwer wrote:

> It is impossible to write about sanctification …
> without taking into account the imitation of

Christ.... The entire life of believers, enveloped as
it is by the demands of sanctification, can be epito-
mized as imitation.[4]

JESUS' HOLINESS IS HIS SINLESSNESS

Holiness is purity, moral perfection, the absence of sin.[5] That to
which we aspire is that which Christ embodied. Seven hundred
years before Christ, the prophet Isaiah, seeing in the Spirit, declared
that the Messiah "committed no sin, and no deceit was found in
his mouth" (1 Peter 2:22; also see Isaiah 53:9). Repeatedly the New
Testament calls Jesus "the Holy One," an Old Testament title used
over thirty times for God himself.

Jesus himself claimed to be sinless.

On one occasion when the Pharisees had been seeking to
undermine him and his ministry, Jesus challenged them: "Can
any of you prove me guilty of sin?" (John 8:46). None could.
But what sort of person claims to be without any sin, without
any fault, and without any guilt whatsoever? No prophet, no
holy man ever made such a bold claim. All who love God know
they fall short of God's standard and being. As has been said, for
Jesus to claim to be without sin makes him demonic, demented,
deluded, or divine.

Jesus' apostles testified to his sinlessness.

Those who knew him best, who lived, ate, slept, and ministered
with him for three years, who had every opportunity to scrutinize

this Jesus—not just the public persona but the private man—could say of him that he was perfect in holiness. Peter said Jesus was "a lamb without blemish or defect," committing no sin, with no deceit coming out of his mouth (1 Peter 1:19; 2:22). John said, "He is pure.… And in him is no sin" (1 John 3:3, 5).

A centurion testified to Jesus' sinlessness.

As Christ breathed his last, and as the very creation protested with earthquake and daytime darkness, a centurion and his soldiers (the very ones who had pierced Christ's side and hammered him to the tree) were terrified, crying out, "Surely he was the Son of God!" (Matt. 27:54). When that ruthless, hardened warrior witnessed how Jesus died, he was led to declare, "Surely this was a righteous man" (Luke 23:47).

The Spirit testifies to Jesus' sinlessness.

We are told that the Spirit's work is to convict the world of guilt in regard to sin, righteousness, and judgment (John 16:8–11), and all three of these are to be interpreted and understood in relation to the person and work of Jesus Christ. Sin is now defined as not believing in Jesus; righteousness is won through Christ rising and ascending and entering the throne room of God the Father; judgment comes from Christ as the judge who stands over the demonic in their condemnation.

The logic of salvation testifies to Jesus' sinlessness.

Jesus is presented as both High Priest and sacrificial Lamb. He is a high priest who offers a sufficient sacrifice that saves utterly because he is "holy, blameless, pure, set apart from sinners, exalted above the heavens. Unlike the other high priests, he does not need to offer sacrifices day after day, first for his own sins, and then for the sins of the people. He sacrificed for their sins once for all when he offered himself" (Heb. 7:26–27). His sacrifice was totally and eternally sufficient because he alone was the spotless sacrifice, offered "unblemished to God" (Heb. 9:14). Death comes through sin. Death could not hold Christ because he was sinless.

JESUS' HOLINESS IS MOVEMENT TOWARD SINNERS

Most holiness cults of Christ's day moved away from sinners, not least the Essenes and the Pharisees. Throughout history, holiness cults have generally been separatist, seeking distance from contamination. But Jesus radically called this concept of purity into question. For a start, he confounded many in the way he came: born to humble parents in a stable rather than to nobility. And he confounded many in his choice of ministry: not to the righteous but to sinners (Matt. 9:13). During his three-year public ministry, Jesus was more likely to be found sharing a meal with prostitutes than with priests, more likely to be theologizing with tax collectors than teachers of the law. The respected religious elite turned his stomach, and he in turn offended their religious sensibilities, earning the label "friend of sinners" (Luke 7:34). Kent Brower understands the motive:

> Time and again the compassion of Jesus for those who are marginalized overrides the legitimate concern for purity.[6]

True holiness always moves toward the sinner, not away. And it does so not in compromise but in compassion. Its desire is always transformation, not condemnation. Divine holiness hates sin, but far from removing itself from sin, it moves toward sin to remove it. Jesus went out of his way to be with sinners—why else would he cross the border into Samaria to meet a woman with a reputation at a well (John 4:1–26)? Why else would he invite himself to tea with a notorious tax collector who robbed his own people and partnered with the enemy (Luke 19:1–9)?

The apostle John tells us, "Do not love the world" (1 John 2:15). This refers to the spirit behind the world and the sinful structures of the world. But for many holiness movements, this verse has sadly been translated into "have nothing to do with sinners"— how un-Christlike is that! To cite the cliché, Jesus truly loved sinners while loathing sin.

One might helpfully speculate where Jesus would be found if he were to pay a visit to this country today. Would he be in the churches or the cafés? In a prayer meeting or a bar? With the clerics or the crowds? I suspect the church leaders would be kept waiting as Christ visited the red-light districts and rescued the abused.

True holiness, true Godlikeness, moves toward sinners, though not toward sin. Holiness is compassionate and cleansing. You cannot cleanse sin if you have nothing to do with sinners. So we must put ourselves in the context and company of sinners without condoning or compromising on sin. Throughout church history, holiness movements have moved away from sinners and society to devote themselves to themselves—to pursue their own purity. This has always been a mistake. True holiness is like salt—penetrating, purifying, preserving, and of no use if it simply stays in its own container

(Matt. 5:13). True holiness, Jesus style, is missional, moving out to sinners and bringing them in to God.

JESUS' HOLINESS PROVOKES THE DEMONIC

At the beginning of his public ministry in Galilee, Jesus entered a synagogue, and a demon immediately manifested itself and shrieked, "What do you want with us, Jesus of Nazareth? Have you come to destroy us? I know who you are—the Holy One of God!" (Mark 1:24). This demon recognized Christ in his humanity (Jesus of Nazareth) and in his divinity (the Holy One of God—the destroyer of demons). This is a clear declaration of holiness.

Why did this demon manifest itself when it did? This was a synagogue, a place of worship. No one knew the man was demonized, unlike the Gadarene demoniac, who had to be chained away from the people (Mark 5). No, this demon lay hidden in the soul of a worshipper until the blazing presence of Christ's purity exposed evil and expelled it with a simple command. Light reveals what was hidden in darkness. The ministry of Jesus was in large part a ministry of deliverance, exorcising the demonic (Mark 1:34). Let us not overlook that in the first few days of Jesus' ministry, there is more reference to the demonic than in the whole of the Old Testament! Why is this? Some would say that a notion of demonology had only just developed in the intertestamental era, and that is why it is a major topic in the Gospels. But surely the intensification of the demonic must be understood as a result of the intensification of the manifest presence of God. The holiness of God was so tangible in Christ that evil couldn't hide. Christ's holiness pierced the darkness. It lifted the stone under which evil was scheming in the dark.

This sinlessness of Jesus is illustrated through his temptations, too. When the Devil sought to make Christ sin in the wilderness, it was not through any overt rebellion and lawlessness but by an oblique undermining of God's Word and God's plan for his life (Matt. 4:1–11). But Christ resisted and rebuked the demonic temptations and subtle machinations. He did so again when Peter sought to keep him from going to Jerusalem, where death awaited him (16:22–23). And his preeminent resistance was seen in the garden of Gethsemane when Jesus begged his Father to remove the cup of suffering and yet chose to follow the will of God over personal interest (26:42).

JESUS' HOLINESS INFURIATES HYPOCRITES

The Pharisees reckoned themselves righteous. They thanked God that they were not as other men. They were the Special Air Service or Navy SEALs of Jewish holiness—God's hard-core pure. Only the most religious, most tenacious, most determined could live up to the demands of the way of the Pharisees, with their laws on laws and rules on rules. They saw themselves as the pinnacle of purity, and everyone agreed they must be. Everyone, that is, except Jesus. He didn't take to their brand of holiness, and they didn't take to his. As we have seen, the Gospels detail the constant conflict between Christ and the Pharisees, essentially a clash of holinesses. Eventually the Pharisees' brand of holiness manipulated, deceived, and bullied its way into killing Christ and, with it, Christ's brand of purity.

True holiness always exposes false holiness. Christ's holiness provoked a crisis because it refused to recognize the pseudoholiness of the religious ruling elite. Christ gave honor where honor was due, and none was due to the Pharisees.

Today the Pharisee still exists, the publicly pious priest or pastor deceived by a self-perceived purity. Such reverends who seek to be revered barely know the Christ of Scripture. God has never looked on outward appearance but ever on the heart. The spirit of the Pharisee, the holy hypocrite, is still the one who honors God with his lips but whose heart is far from him, the one who worships God in vain with nothing more than human teachings (Matt. 15:8). That is how hypocrisy reacts to the holy.

Happily, the converse is true: When someone sincerely longs for holiness and pursues it, they will recognize Christ as its perfection and personification and not find it hard to embrace him and follow hard after him.

JESUS' HOLINESS UPS THE BAR ON RIGHTEOUSNESS

The strange thing is that, while the Pharisee thought Jesus undermined the law and the rabbinical interpretation of it, while the Pharisee thought Christ trod the sacred in the dust, causing Moses to turn in his grave, Jesus in fact intensified the demands of the law. Far from being lowered, the bar was raised. What was a high jump became a pole vault under Christ. Jesus was no antinomian—someone who says the law is no longer relevant now that we are under grace.

I recall visiting the sacred site in Galilee where Christ is thought to have given the Sermon on the Mount (one of the more probable historical sites in the Holy Land). Our saintly guide took me aside and told me that he had once brought a group here and they had read from the Sermon on the Mount. While several thought it beautiful, the height of moral instruction—blessed ethics—one young man reacted with, "That is vicious!" Surprised, our guide pressed him, and he declared that the demands of Christ were unattainable and demanded way too much of mere human beings.

The young man was right about one thing—Jesus demanded a righteousness that "surpasse[d] that of the Pharisees" (Matt. 5:20). Jesus repeatedly quoted the Law of Moses, "You have heard that it was said…" only to intensify its demands: "But I tell you.…" He made more strict the law on murder, saying hatred in one's heart would be judged like murder; on adultery, saying lust in one's mind would be judged as the physical transgression; on divorce, saying there were almost no grounds permissible for it. Jesus taught that his followers should pray, fast, give sacrificially, and, most demanding of all, love their neighbors as themselves—all of their neighbors, especially the ones they would naturally hate (Matt. 5—7)!

So yes, Jesus' holiness raised the bar on the law: He expected more from his followers, not less, than the Pharisees. Yet at the same time, Jesus' love, wed to his holiness, gave grace to those who failed the standard while not compromising on it. True holiness as Christ lived and taught is not an unattainable bar to beat us with—it is Christlikeness, and all who know and love him will seek to be like him. Holiness will be a destiny of delight, not duty. Christ himself will provide the pole to do the vault.

JESUS' HOLINESS CONFRONTS HINDRANCES TO THE HOLY

On entering the temple, Jesus saw the money changers' benches and the traders and buyers (Matt. 21:12–13), and he was filled with righteous indignation. People were profiting out of prayer. People were ripping off those who desired to come and meet God. Hurdles were placed in the way, tripping up the sincere. Access to God's temple was difficult if you weren't wealthy. The temple priest cults were businessmen—didn't the building have high running costs? Temple taxes needed to be paid in Jewish currency because the common Roman coinage depicting Caesars were unclean, even blasphemous. But that wasn't all: There was money to be made by those who converted the peasants' denarii into shekels—the money changers.

The humble pilgrim, only too conscious of his sin, had to offer a sacrifice of doves or a lamb. But he couldn't bring his own—no, he had to buy a spotless offering, one deemed acceptable by the temple priests. And where could you buy such an offering, approved by the priests? From the priests, of course! Another opportunity for profit—charging vastly inflated prices for the approved animal.

We shouldn't be surprised, then, when Christ enters, that his righteous rage breaks out like a volcanic eruption. Turning over the tables, whipping out the marketeers, he shouts, "'My house will be called a house of prayer,' but you are making it a 'den of robbers'" (Matt. 21:13).

The holy place for prayer had been defiled. The holy pursuit of pilgrims had been turned into quick profit. The poor are always the ones least able to pay, and this meant their devotion to God was restricted. Those priests who were ordained to represent God had merely represented their own self-interest—and in the process brought a slur on God's name and his house. There is an anger which is not sin—hence the injunction to "be angry and do not sin" of Ephesians 4:26 (ESV). Jesus was angry, and he had every right to be. Holiness is angered at unholiness that goes by the name of holiness. Woe to those popes, prelates, priests, pastors, and preachers who use their position for their own gain, who manipulate the sincere devotion of others for their own ends. The minister will be judged most severely.

JESUS' HOLINESS RESCUES UNHOLY SINNERS

We have noted that holiness moves toward sinners and removes the demonic. Ultimately, if sin is to be eradicated, it must be judged, God's wrath against it satisfied, and its stain on life wiped clean. Christ's holiness is seen in his sufficient substitution for sinners. Paul said, "God made him who had no sin to be sin for us, so that in him we might become the righteousness of God" (2 Cor. 5:21). Christ could be no substitute if he were a sinner himself—only an offering without blemish will be acceptable for sin. And so the beloved Son of God, blameless and spotless, in love for sinners and in hatred of sin, "poured out his soul to death and was numbered with the transgressors; yet he bore the sin of many, and makes intercession for the transgressors" (Isa. 53:12 ESV).

Kent Brower sums up:

> For Jesus, holiness is contagious, outgoing, embracing and joyous. It transforms and brings reconciliation.[7]

The pseudoholiness of the Pharisees, and all religions, places burdens on people. The holiness of Jesus removes burdens, and he takes those burdens on himself. Christ's holiness does not point a finger at our sin and guilt; he takes it in his nail-scarred hands and crushes it. God's true holiness is love that identifies with sinners. It is love that embraces sinners, and love that bids them welcome.

Chapter 9

Wanted: Dead and Alive

For you died, and your life is now hidden with Christ in God.... Put to death, therefore, whatever belongs to your earthly nature. (Col. 3:3, 5)

We have come a long way on our journey. We have seen the foundation of holiness in God himself, the absence of holiness in sin, the misplaced longing for holiness in religion, and the provision of true holiness in Jesus and faith in him. In the remaining chapters, we turn our attention to the practicalities of holiness, the "yes, but how?"

SINNERS SIN, AND SO DO SAINTS—BUT SINNERS DON'T MIND, AND SAINTS DO

The inescapable fact of the Christian life is that Christians sin. Though many regret this and seek to live otherwise, repeatedly they fall into old patterns of thinking and acting according to the desires and dictates of the flesh, which they know are the very things that crucified Christ. Best effort, determination, spiritual disciplines—all often seem unable to bring victory. Many people groan, *Will I ever be free, holy as God is holy?*

The great twentieth-century theologian Karl Barth once spoke for many when he asked:

> I, who am a Christian, can I really live ... according to my faith and in obedience? Shall I be able to live thus in the midst of the necessities of my existence?—Yes, according to the gospel it is possible in the holiness of obedience to live that which is given us to live, that which we must live.[1]

Can the very power, presence, and propensity to sin be broken? I believe the answer to that question is yes, and I believe the answer to the next question, "But how?" is found in Romans 6.[2]

UNITED TO CHRIST

The renowned twentieth-century Bible teacher Dr. Martyn Lloyd-Jones described Romans 6 as the most liberating passage in the Bible. Yet for many years he steered clear of it, and once when asked by a famous preacher when he would preach a series on Romans, he replied immediately, "Not until I understand Romans 6."[3] Some years later, feeling he had finally grasped it, he produced his famous life's work on Romans.

Romans 6 certainly is a demanding passage, but if we can rightly divine its meaning and practically apply its truths, we will find liberation from sin, for Romans 6 presents us with Paul's understanding of the relationship of the Christian to sin and deliverance from it.

Lloyd-Jones stated its importance thus:

> Here, then, is the doctrine that is before us, the doctrine of our union with Christ. Once more we must say that it is one of the most glorious aspects of the Christian truth, one of the most profound, one of the most stimulating, one of the most comforting—indeed I rather like to use the word exhilarating. There is nothing, perhaps, in the whole range and realm of doctrine which, if properly grasped and understood, gives greater assurance, greater comfort, and greater hope than this doctrine of our union with Christ.[4]

As we look at Romans 6, we shall focus on the implications of union with Christ and highlight the key stepping-stones through the text that indicate why and how we may live a new life. We shall discover how this union through faith and baptism is a very real union with his dying and rising, an actual and objective state that establishes a new identity for the believer and, with it, a new direction for the moral life and a new power over sin as we live in conformity to Christ.

Paul named, shamed, and aimed at sin. Romans 6 and 7 are about the believer's struggle with sin. Paul never shied away from the real nitty-gritty of the Christian life. He was no Victorian prude whose politeness didn't permit the mention of sin. He did not seek to conceal the issue of sin in the church but rather to reveal it, bringing it into the light and dealing with it according to the gospel. Many of us Christians are kept in bondage to sin simply because we won't bring it into the light and deal with it before God. Hidden sin won't go away, and so Paul went for it head-on.

SIN IS SURROUNDED

Sin is hemmed in. Christ crucified has annulled its penalty and broken its power. Romans 5:1 tells us we have *justification*. Romans 8:1 tells us we have *no condemnation*. No matter what sins I may have done or what sin I still may do, the determining reality in my life is what Christ has done, dying for me at Calvary, and what Christ will do, standing for me on judgment day. Whatever the ongoing operation of sin in the believer's life, it is temporal and without eternal consequence. It may accuse, but it cannot condemn. It has no power to undo what God has done. Sin cannot rob me of my rights. It cannot reverse God's decree and declaration over my life. It is an irritant whose days are numbered. Whatever its presence, its power in my life is broken, its penalty covered. It seeks to undermine God's work in me and God's will for me—but it cannot cancel out my new true identity as one united with Christ, or my security of eternity with Christ.

THERE IS GRACE FOR SIN

Paul said (Rom. 5:20) that where sin increased, grace abounded all the more. Grace smothers sin. Whatever hand sin throws down on the table, God's royal flush wins. Grace marches out to meet and defeat sin.

Romans 6:1 begins with the question: "Are we to continue in sin so that grace may increase?" Now, grace reveals God's character and brings God glory. Something good comes out of something bad; so a few Roman Christians mused, "May we do bad so the good can come?" Paul's answer was unequivocal—no (6:2)! Grace is the provision for sin but never permission for sin. One thinks of the oft-repeated caricature of the Roman Catholic who sins all week knowing he can go to confession and absolution on Friday. Ironically, were that true, at least it would show an awareness of grace. Luther infamously said,

> God does not save people who are only fictitious sin-
> ners.... [S]in boldly, but believe and rejoice in Christ
> even more boldly, for he is victorious over sin.[5]

Sin boldly? Luther was not telling people to sin, intentionally setting his theology at odds with Paul; he was underscoring that, even *if* we commit great and gross sin, God's grace is sufficient to forgive it.

PAUL NEVER CONCEDED A WIN TO SIN

Paul admitted sin but never gave in to it. He assumed we will wage war against sin—we will never yield to it, never surrender to it. Never did Paul consider sin might win, not for an instant. It is a power already defeated by the resurrection. No terms are to be given to it. The whole tone of Romans 6, therefore, is one of hope. Victory is assumed. We recall the speech given by Winston Churchill at his old school, where he thundered:

> This is the lesson: never give in, never give in, never,
> never, never, never—in nothing, great or small,
> large or petty—never give in except to convictions
> of honor and good sense. Never yield to force;
> never yield to the apparently overwhelming might
> of the enemy.[6]

Never giving in to sin requires knowing how to live in union with Christ.

THE SAT NAV TO SANCTIFICATION

Romans 6 begins with the question of sin and ends with the expectation of holiness. The spiritual Romans 6 Sat Nav, or GPS, starts with present location "shall we sin?" and ends with destination "holiness." Throughout, Paul directs us along the main highways to holiness. Twice he spoke of our response to sin and our pursuit of righteousness, "resulting in sanctification" (vv. 19, 22). Paul believed we will get there; that holiness is not wishful thinking but is the result of right acting. Paul clearly believed sanctification, holiness, and practical righteousness is realistic; it is attainable. The Christian journey is heading toward holiness. At times on the journey, there may be delays, diversions, or even breakdowns. But just as a Sat Nav recalibrates position constantly and directs us forward, so the Holy Spirit directs us to our destination.

INDICATIVES AND IMPERATIVES

The structure of Romans 6 moves between indicatives (who we are) and imperatives (what we must do). The imperatives are possible only because of the indicatives. We are unable to do what God requires us to do until we understand who we are in Christ; or, put more positively, we are able to do what God requires when we understand who we are in Christ. Our actions are determined by our being. Paul constantly reminded believers of their identity and, in light of that, their responsibility. He underscored what God has made us before telling us what we need to do. As Christians, we are often defeated from the start by sin because we do not know who we are in Christ. We do not understand that we are new creations—no longer slaves but sons.

As Paul later wrote, if you think you are a slave, you will live like a slave—but if you know you are God's son or daughter, the child who inherits, you will act accordingly (Gal. 4:1–7). Paul always structured his letters this way—helping us understand our new being and then moving to our new doing. We are in Christ, moving toward total conformity with his morally perfect life. We move from holiness *in* him to holiness *like* him.

UNITED TO CHRIST MEANS WE LIVE A NEW LIFE

Paul tells us that, through baptism in water and the spiritual reality that symbolizes, we have been united with Christ in his crucifixion (Rom. 6:6), in his death (v. 3), in his burial (v. 4), and in his resurrection (vv. 4–5). He stated, "As Christ was raised from the dead through the glory of the Father, so we too might walk in newness of life" (v. 4). For Paul, the resurrection life was not just a hope for the future but a present reality today that affects the believer's moral life—the new life we may live is a life free from the sin that marked the old life. In the Greek, he was literally saying that now "we may walk in a new way." We are still living in Adam's body, not yet clothed in our resurrected body; nevertheless now, today, united to Christ, already the resurrection power of the Spirit is at work to enable a morally transformed way of living.

WE HAVE DIED

Paul said, "We have died with Christ" (v. 8). But in what sense have we died with Christ?[7]

First, we have died in the *baptismal* sense—our baptism symbolizes our identification and union by faith with Christ.

Second, we have certainly died in the *judicial* sense—God has judged our sins in Christ and reckons his death as sufficient substitute for our deserved death.

But third, we have also died in a *moral* sense—Christ's death for sin is also a protest, a divine *no* to sin, and our faith in Christ affirms this no. My death with Christ involves a very real change in my being. Becoming a new creation requires a transformation of the old creation, a very real separation from who I was "in Adam." The new life comes through the death of the old. That death is not simply judicial but transformational. Paul spoke of this transformation as a death to the old life and receiving of a new life, and a key indicator in the change from death to life is in my relationship to sin: I am not simply forgiven but able to come out from under sin's control.

Before I became a Christian, I was in Adam's race, and sin had a very real grip on me. But now I am dead to Adam and alive to Christ, and sin no longer has a judicial claim over me; nor does it have a moral hold over me. I am free from its condemnation and can be free from its control. Sin reigned in our old nature, our former self, but

the sinner under God's wrath died to sin, died to Adam, was crucified with Christ, was judged with Christ, and was raised with him
to a new life under a new head. Sin was a key feature of our old life
in Adam, but by union with Christ we have died to all we inherited
from Adam—in particular, sin's propensity and power (v. 2).

Paul tells us we died to sin (v. 6). In the Greek, he literally said
that "our old man"—our old self—was crucified with Jesus in order
that our body of sin—this present flawed flesh and blood—might be
done away with. As a result, we are no longer slaves to sin. Whoever
has died is freed from sin (v. 7).

The eminent New Testament scholar C. E. B. Cranfield put\ it
this way:

> The death to sin which Christians are here said to
> have died is, according to Paul, an event which
> has rendered their continuing in sin as something
> essentially absurd.[8]

It makes no sense to sin, as one who has died to it. That's why
Lloyd-Jones said that the Christian who sins is a fool! We who are
dead to sin, who have crucified the old self inherited from Adam that
was under God's judgment, are now to live as resurrected believers in
the power of the resurrection, by the Spirit of God.

The great commentators Sanday and Headlam go as far as to say
this:

> The Baptised Christian cannot sin. Sin is a direct
> contradiction of the state of things which baptism

assumes … As Christ by his death on the cross
ceased from all contact with sin, so the Christian,
united with Christ in his baptism, has done once
and for all with sin, and lives henceforth a reformed
life, dedicated to God.[9]

They add the caveat that this non-sinning is the ideal, whatever
the reality in the Christian's life may be. I for one am grateful they
add that, otherwise many of us would be left feeling condemned,
knowing a very real ongoing war with sin where we don't win every
battle. While Paul believed there was a very real transformation of
our humanity through union with Christ, it is all a work in progress.
Though we are renewed in Christ, we still wrestle with sin in our
fallen flesh and in our fallen world. In his first letter, John pointed
out this tension between the ideal—"no one … will continue to sin"
(1 John 3:9)—and the real—"if anyone does sin" (2:1).

NO LONGER SLAVES

United with Christ, Christians are freed from sin—free from its
condemnation, its contamination, and its control. Paul was sure
the power that once dominated our lives and made us its victims—
against which we were as powerless as puppets—has in fact been
broken. The temptation to return to sin remains present (until
Christ's return) because we live in a sinful world; we have bodies
with minds in which sin has been programmed, but we are no longer
its whipping boys, following its whim. Whereas it once had power
over my very being, now, as a new being in Christ, I have power over
it. Adam is no longer the major determinate; Christ is.

How often do you hear someone confessing his or her sin only to almost justify it by adding, "But I couldn't help it!"? The Christian who is dead with Christ and therefore dead to sin *can* help it. Not only does Jesus cancel sin's debt, but, as Charles Wesley so beautifully wrote,

> He breaks the power of cancelled sin—he sets the prisoner free.[10]

DEATH DUTIES

Indicatives lead to imperatives. Jesus' death for our sin and our death to our sin bring us to a place of responsibility. There are death duties to pay. Paul's choice of verbs indicates the believer's present identity in union with Christ is to be followed by real and practical requirements to live without sin. Being "dead, baptized, buried, crucified, united, freed" brings responsibilities:

- "Consider yourselves to be dead to sin, but alive to God" (Rom. 6:11).
- "Do not let sin reign in your mortal body so that you obey its lusts" (v. 12).
- "Do not go on presenting the members of your body to sin as instruments of unrighteousness ..." (v. 13).
- "but present yourselves to God as those alive from the dead ..." (v. 13).
- "and [present] your members as instruments of righteousness to God" (v. 13).

What is immediately apparent from these verses is the responsibility that is placed on us to walk in freedom from sin. Nowhere is there the suggestion, as some spiritualities and theologies have encouraged, that sinless perfection is the result of a second blessing, a perfection of love. Nowhere is there even a hint that all I have to do is believe I am dead and, by some exercise of faith in that death, never sin again. This list of very active verbs makes it clear that action is required on our part to overcome sin. The fact that two of the verbs (not letting sin reign, not presenting our members to sin) are in the present tense suggests the need for *ongoing* activity and tenacity to resist the pressure of sin. It is clear that Paul was appealing to Christians to enact and apply the will to these things—he told them what to do and what not to do. So there is a "doing." Let us look at them a little more closely.

> *Consider yourselves to be dead to sin, but alive to God.*
> *(v. 11)*

The key word here, translated "consider," is *logizomai.* This has a range of meanings and conveys the general sense of "to reckon, to count, to compute, to calculate, to take into account." This is not an act of pretending or wishful thinking, not an "as if" but "a deliberate and sober judgment" of reality.[11] Christians are to constantly know themselves in the sight of the gospel—to look at their account, their standing with God—and to see that they are in fact crucified with Christ, dead to their old life, dead to sin, and risen with Christ to a new life. *Logizomai* has an almost mathematical, even financial connotation: "Do the math, look at the numbers, examine the accounts." As a Christian, see your transaction with God.

So we must daily, constantly, intelligently, reasonably, and logically remind ourselves of who we are and how we must live. We *are* dead to sin; we *are* alive to God; we *do* live in the power of the resurrection. When tempted to sin, we must consider how we came to be dead to sin—it cost God the death of his own dear Son.

This reckoning of my old self as crucified with Christ is not the end to dealing with sin. In Christ I have died to the law and to its accusation and condemnation. But I also have the responsibility to tackle head-on the remaining "yeast" of sin that remains at work in the body I have inherited from Adam. My failure of God's moral law is satisfied by Christ's death, but that annuls neither the moral law nor my responsibility to abide by it. Now, dead to sin and alive to Christ by the indwelling Spirit, I am in fact able to fulfill its decrees.

Do not let sin reign in your mortal body so that you obey its lusts. (v. 12)

Paul envisaged sin as a power working in us, leading us to commit sinful acts. Sin will try to get the upper hand and make us act in disobedience. After all, before we met Christ, sin was used to being in control because of our descent from Adam. But now we are united with Jesus. Someone else reigns now, not sin—we have been transferred from the kingdom of darkness into the kingdom of light. We have thrown out the puppet king, Satan, and now follow King Jesus. Sin's sphere of influence is in our flesh, the mortal bodies we must carry around until we are clothed with immortality. Sin seeks to express its reign, but that is now the reign of a usurper, and the only right to rule that it can have is the right we assent to.

When I was a student pastor, I occasionally shocked someone seeking counsel by my advice. If they confessed a habitual sin, and I felt that there were no deeper issues beyond their own control, I would say, "Just stop it. Don't do it!" That's Paul's advice—no pandering to cultural context or social custom or personal preference. No, says Paul; just stop it!

> *Do not go on presenting the members of your body to*
> *sin as instruments of unrighteousness … (v. 13)*

The word *members* refers to our physical parts. We are not to use our minds to conceive sin, our eyes to lust, our tongues to curse and lie, our ears to listen to wickedness, our feet to walk toward evil, or our hands to reach out to it. The term Paul used for *presenting* joins together the ideas of "standing" and "being next to"; the term translated *instruments* refers to tools or weapons. So we are not to stand next to sin; we are not to go near it; and we are not to provide it with the weapons that can bring about our own downfall.

> *but present yourselves to God … and your members as*
> *instruments of righteousness. (v. 13)*

Rather, we are to "stand before God" and live our lives facing him. Holiness is a life lived facing God. There is a divine either/or here—but many waver between two opinions and two actions, serving God and Baal, light and darkness, wanting to offer the members of their bodies to both God and to the rule of sin through the flesh.

No, said Paul—do not present any part of your body to sin, but present every part of your body to God. The dead man walks in the spirit opposite to that of the sinful man. The result makes a very practical difference—elsewhere Paul gave examples: the person who used to steal "must steal no longer, but … work"; "unwholesome talk" should give way to words that edify (Eph. 4:28–29).

Sin in a Christian's life is evidence that part of his or her flesh has been offered as an instrument for unrighteousness instead of righteousness. That person has sided with sin. This offering is not a feeling or a sentiment but a habit or an act of the will. The more you do it, the more you become accustomed to it. The more you offer a bodily member to sin, the more power that sin will have over you. By the same token, the more you offer your members to righteousness, the more holiness will be a way of life and not a "work." Just as sin becomes a habit, so can holiness. It will be the fruit of habitually offering your will to conform to God's will. Paul spoke in Galatians 6:8 of two cycles of life—the vicious cycle of sin from sowing to the flesh and the virtuous cycle of life from sowing to the Spirit.

The distinguished evangelist David MacInnes told me of an incident when a pastor from behind the former Iron Curtain attended a conference in Britain. This pastor stated that whenever he saw a police car he would panic, reexperiencing the fear from the days when the Stasi, the German secret police, were known to arrest, imprison, and torture Christians. Though free from that power, he was still dogged by it. He needed to retrain his automatic fear responses. He was a slave to fear. We are free from the condemnation of sin—we need to live free from the influence of sin.

For sin shall not be master over you, for you are not under law but under grace. (Rom. 6:14)

Paul concluded this section with hope. Sin is not our master, and we are not its slaves. Its tyranny is broken, its penalty cancelled, its power defeated, even though we still experience its presence. "Sin shall not be master over you" is not a command; it is a promise—more, it is a statement of what is now true. Sin will have no dominion over you—no rule, no authority, no power, no mastery. That is the promise here. William Greathouse said,

> Paul does not mean that Christians have become incapable of sinning. By the grace of God and the power of the Spirit they are able not to sin. This does not mean they are unable to sin.[12]

We are no longer under the law, which pointed its finger at our sin but didn't lift a finger to help us. In fact, Paul said, the law actually exacerbated our appetite for sin. The law cannot control sin; it can only reveal it. We are under the new covenant of grace—grace that shows us God's love for us; grace that beckons to us; grace that has paid the price for our sin; grace that stoops, stays, and strengthens us to walk free from sin. We are not facing the power of sin singlehandedly; we face it in God's *charis,* his grace gift.

YOU GOTTA SERVE SOMEBODY

In Romans 6:15–22, Paul introduced a fresh argument but made the same point. He opened with the same question he began with in 6:1—"What then? Shall we sin ...?" and again he answered unequivocally, "May it never be!" Don't even go there—don't even think about it. This is the opposite of "Amen." Paul barked out a *no!* to any notion that we may give up or give in to sin. There should be no willful continuance in sin. Paul's emphatic "No, you may not sin" must surely hold hope that "No, we might not sin." The command holds within it the possibility of fulfillment—if it didn't, the command would be just more law that condemns. And as we saw in verse 14, we are not under law but under the power of grace.

In verses 16–22, Paul continued the theme of presenting our bodily members to sin or to God, comparing the choice to slavery. The one who presents himself to sin is a slave to unrighteousness. The one who presents himself to God is a slave to God. Though they were once slaves to sin, now, having obeyed the teaching of the gospel, they have been freed from sin—freed from its penalty and its power, if not its presence. Sin enslaved us before we met Christ and would still like to enslave us and rob us of the virtues of being in Christ. If we give in to sin, we do so absurdly—as free men who offer ourselves to enslavement! But it is ours to decide whom we will serve. We have freedom—will we offer ourselves to God or to sin?

DEAD IN CHRIST—SO PUT TO DEATH

Okay. I am united with Christ. I died with him and am raised with him. But, practically speaking, am I free from sinning? Have you ever met a Christian who was completely conformed to Christ, enslaved to righteousness? I confess I have never met a sinless Christian; I have never met anyone who was so dead to sin that his or her whole life was lived to God.

I don't think Paul had, either. In Galatians 2:20, Paul said, "I have been crucified with Christ"; and yet, practically, he wrote, "I die every day" (1 Cor. 15:31) and, "I want to know Christ and the power of his resurrection and the fellowship of sharing in his sufferings, becoming like him in his death" (Phil. 3:10). Every day, we are to struggle to live in total submission to the will of God, total conformity to the character of Christ, total obedience to the leading of the Spirit.

Now, some see a potential contradiction in this theme—how can we at the same time be "dead to sin" and be instructed to "put to death" or "reckon ourselves dead"? What does it mean to have died with Christ and be dead to sin when the evidence suggests sin is very much alive even in the believer? Has there been a real dying, or is this metaphor purely judicial?

I believe it is a mystery, but one Paul held to firmly. There is a very real dying of my old nature with Christ, a very real union with Christ in death, a very real rising and living a new life in Christ by the Spirit. This dying affects my whole nature and not merely my moral status, as does my being raised and living in Christ. Nevertheless, something of the old life casts a shadow into the new. And so there is a pattern from the past that must be put to death in the present so we have strength to resist temptation.

John Stott has attempted to steer us through the dialectic:

> There are, in fact, two quite distinct ways in which the New Testament speaks of crucifixion in relation to holiness. The first is our death to sin through identification with Christ; the second is our death to self through imitation of Christ. On the one

hand, we have been crucified with Christ. But on
the other we have crucified … our sinful nature
with all its desires.… The first is a legal death, a
death to the penalty of sin; the second is a moral
death, a death to the power of sin.[13]

The first of these took place in the past by means of our union
with Christ's death for us, through faith and baptism. The second
takes place in the present through our daily crucifying of the flesh.
The basis for our crucifying present sin in the flesh is the very real
dying with Christ that went before.

What might this look like? There is a powerful and practical
example in the life of Billy Graham. He said that he had no problem with attraction to other women, declaring himself to be dead
to every woman but his wife, Ruth. But he didn't just declare that
truth—he lived in the light of it. And so a more careful minister I
have never heard of, never in all his years taking a room in a hotel
without sharing with a male colleague and never allowing himself to
be alone in a room with a woman when the door was closed. Was
he dead to every woman, once and for all; or did he die daily and in
a disciplined manner to every woman other than Ruth? The answer,
clearly, is both.

When I gave my life to Jesus as Lord and Savior, it did seem
I was a totally new creation. The old had gone, and the new had
come. It was clear there were many things that I had died to—I
stopped smoking instantly, and no foul language came out of my
mouth again. Immediately, certain passions and desires were gone. It
seemed as if I was truly dead to sin and alive to God.

But other sins did not die. They were still there to haunt me and taunt me. Lusts of the flesh, attitudes of the heart, programs of the mind ... the old sinful Simon, though crucified with Christ, seemed to be present with me. And seeds of sins I didn't even exhibit as a young adult have flowered in my flesh. There is clearly a need to die daily, as Paul said. Daily, weekly, monthly, the Lord reveals latent sins of the flesh that must be brought to the cross and crucified. Yes, I am a new creation, but in my old body with my old mind. The difference is that now, by union with Christ, the power and pattern of sin in body and mind can be overcome.

I like the amusing story of the famous Baptist preacher C. H. Spurgeon, who was seen leaving a voting booth. Someone remarked, "I thought you were a citizen of heaven!" To this he replied, "I am, but my old man is a Tory!"

You know you are dead to something when it doesn't hurt to give it up or when you don't take offense if someone does you wrong. By contrast, your flesh is still very much alive in you if you have to fight tooth and nail to rid yourself of something or if you take offense when wronged. My godly colleague Gordon Hickson says you are dead when your flesh doesn't rise: "Dead men don't have toes to step on." We are dead when we don't react in the flesh to any hurt or offense, when we don't seek to justify ourselves, satisfy ourselves, live for ourselves. The quicker we lie down (in Christ) and die, the less painful it will be.

Our fallen flesh will be very much here until we receive our resurrection bodies, so it is here that sins must be done to death, where the contest is fought out between our redeemed souls and our fallen flesh. Some have even claimed a victory over sin as if by a postconversion death. But Paul said we already have died, not that we need to die "to enter into the experience." We need to reckon ourselves as dead and live in the reality of that death and the new life in Christ by the Spirit, which replaces the old life. What is needed is not a postconversion death but rather a postconversion reckoning of being dead to sin. This opens the door to a constant living partnership with the Spirit in daily resisting sin and offering the body to acts of righteousness.

I suspect many of those who speak of a one-off death after conversion have in mind more of a revelation of being dead with Christ to sin, a resolution to live in Christ rather than in the flesh. Such a revelation of our position as dead to sin and alive to Christ would undoubtedly need a moment-by-moment ratification. The sad thing is many Christians don't truly understand their new identity in Christ and so continue in sin rather than growing in conformity to Christ.

Again I must say that, during two decades of following hard after Christ, I have yet to meet someone so dead to sin that he or she never commits sin. During two decades of reading Christian biographies of the great saints, I have never read of a truly perfected person in this life. I do not believe anyone is entirely sanctified, free from sin as the result of one day's decision or death. But I do believe that many have known a day when they realized and reckoned (as John Gregory Mantle wrote) that:

> "On the Cross He was crucified for me," and "On the Cross I am crucified with Him." The one aspect brings us deliverance from sin's condemnation and the other from sin's power.[14]

And ever thereafter they have sought to live, not just thankfully that Christ died for their sins, but practically walking in union with Christ, seeking to live as he did.

There is no secret to sanctification, no momentary experience of the Spirit bringing us to a total experience of entire perfection, no crisis of surrender or act of faith ushering us straight into a victorious life. Holiness is a provision through the cross whereby Christ was crucified for me and I was crucified with him because I am placed in him. At that cross, the power, penalty, and permanence of sin were dealt with. By faith and baptism, the old sinner Simon died with Christ and, perhaps more important, was raised with him by the Spirit. This is not just a symbol; it is actual. Simon the sinner has been crucified with Christ and may no longer live except with Christ living in me (Gal. 2:20), in the power of the resurrection (Eph. 1:19–20) and the power of the Spirit (Eph. 3:16).

And in that power, I am being transformed into the likeness of Christ as I daily submit my life to God, daily conforming my will to his, daily reckoning myself dead to sin, daily giving no room for sin in my members, daily offering myself to God, daily using my members for righteousness, daily abandoning myself as God's slave.

Daily growing in holiness.

Chapter 10
Holy Spirit, Holy Living

Gordon Fee said this of the human body:

> It is sanctified by the presence of God himself
> through the Holy Spirit. We must therefore sanctify
> it as well, by living the life in the Spirit, a life of
> holiness.[1]

We have seen that Paul appealed to the will—he very clearly commanded us, with powerful imperatives, not to sin but to act righteously. He assumed that the new man in Christ has the ability to comprehend and respond to this. No longer subject to sin, we have power over sin, and we can take authority and act to eradicate the habitual patterns of sin in our mind and flesh, perfecting our life into the likeness of Christ.[2]

That said, Paul definitely didn't think that God has done his bit (removing sin's power and penalty) and simply left us to do our bit (removing sin's presence) without any help. Whereas our salvation was a purely solo event on God's part, to which we could add nothing, our sanctification is a joint affair, in which we partner with God in our transformation into Christlikeness. God is still very much at work.

Paul moved from speaking of our death in Romans 6 and 7 to telling us of our new life in Romans 8, a life in the Spirit. The Spirit, while not mentioned directly in Romans 6, is nevertheless active, for the Spirit is the power that raised Jesus from the dead, and the Spirit revivifies our dead spirit and now resides in us. It is this Holy Spirit who partners with us in perfecting our path in and toward holiness.

The Holy Spirit is the presupposition of our holy life. Paul often used the term *glory* as a synonym for the Holy Spirit, and he tells us that Christ was raised from the dead by the glory of the Father (Rom. 6:4). The Holy Spirit is the power of the resurrection (Rom. 1:4), and that same glorious power lives in us (Eph. 1:19–20). Ninety times in the New Testament the Spirit is called Holy. Perhaps it is a primary predicate of the Spirit because it is the primary role of the Spirit to make us holy. The Holy Spirit is the sanctifying Spirit.

A while ago, I had a cycle accident and severely smashed my knee, crushing my tibia. Surgeons placed a large cobalt rod along the break, glued the many smashed pieces together, and secured them with seven bolts. Slowly, my leg has healed and fused to the metal rod, which has remolded the leg in the right position, enabling me to walk again. In a similar manner, sin is like a terrible crippling accident (although, unlike my accident, it's our fault). God the surgeon places his Holy Spirit within us to straighten and strengthen us. As we gradually conform and build our lives around him, we are enabled to walk rightly, in holiness.

THE SPIRIT CHANGES US AS WE LET HIM

The Old Testament prophets made this connection with holiness as they anticipated the indwelling Spirit. Ezekiel delivered God's promise:

> *I will give them one heart, and a new spirit I will put within them. I will remove the heart of stone from their flesh and give them a heart of flesh, that they may walk in my statutes and keep my rules and obey them. (11:19–20 ESV)*

Sanctification equals you and me walking in God's statutes through the gift of a new spirit. There is an ambiguity here—was Ezekiel speaking of the human spirit or the Holy Spirit? The prophet resolved this in chapter 36 when he spoke of God giving a new human spirit by the work of his divine Spirit:

> *I will sprinkle clean water on you, and you will be clean; I will cleanse you from all your impurities and from all your idols. I will give you a new heart and put a new spirit in you; I will remove from you your heart of stone and give you a heart of flesh. And I will put my Spirit in you and move you to follow my decrees and be careful to keep my laws. (vv. 25–27)*

The prophet proclaimed a time when the Holy Spirit would dwell within all his people and soften their hard hearts, enabling them to walk according to God's laws—to walk in holiness and righteousness. We as Christians live in that promise. The indwelling Spirit of God has cleansed us from our sin, given us a new heart, and now seeks to conform us to Christ. Yet how often are we happy to be cleansed from the guilt of our sin, only to show reluctance in following God's decrees? Andrew Murray was right to say that it's a sick Christian who is happy to have life by the Spirit but not walk in the Spirit.[3]

This was the problem with the Galatian church. Having started in the Spirit, having received the Spirit (Gal. 3:2), they thought they could go it alone. They were no doubt grateful to the Spirit for sprinkling them clean but then didn't rely on the Spirit to move them to follow and be careful to keep God's laws. Many Christians get into serious difficulties and remain trapped for years in sinful habits and mind-sets because they have received the Spirit for regeneration (sprinkled clean by water—see Ezekiel 36:25) but are not prepared to walk in the Spirit for sanctification (moved to keep God's law—see Ezekiel 36:27). They try to keep the law as the Galatians did—in their own power—and wonder why they fall flat on their faces.

When Samuel anointed Saul as king over Israel, he declared, "The Spirit of the LORD will come upon you in power, and you will prophesy with them; and you will be changed into a different person" (1 Sam. 10:6). Tragically, having received the Spirit, and having received the charism of prophecy, too, Saul did not allow the Holy Spirit to transform him and conform him to God's law; consequently he lost his life through rebellion.

Clearly we need to grasp this understanding of the Spirit as bringing change to character as well as through charisma. Tragically, the charismatic church has sought charisms—"you will proph-esy"—while often failing to welcome being "changed into a different person." Many want the charisms of the Spirit without the character. This was true of the Corinthian church to whom the apostle Paul wrote. They lacked no charismatic gift of the Spirit (1 Cor. 1:7) but seemed to be missing every Holy Spirit character trait; so he rebuked them for being immoral, divisive, idolatrous, and arrogant. And today ... how many want the Holy Spirit power for works of service but not for walks in Christlikeness? Do we have our eyes on ourselves rather than God's glory?

THE SPIRIT DOWN THE AGES

The church fathers in their theology gave little attention to sanctifica-tion by the Spirit, due mainly to the fact that their attention focused on fighting heresy and heterodoxy on various fronts that generally were to do with teaching about Christ. However, Athanasius, noted for his stance against the heresy of Arianism (the belief that Jesus was not God), also defended the Trinity and so the deity of the Holy Spirit. Athanasius' argument was that Scripture reveals the Spirit to be the Sanctifier. If becoming holy is becoming like God, then the Spirit who makes us holy must be God; only a divine person can work a divine effect. Athanasius's purpose was to prove the divinity of the Spirit, but in so doing, he underlined that the activity of the Spirit is to make us holy.

The Reformers, for their part, wanted to exorcise holiness from any medieval hint of "works righteousness," whereby we make our-selves righteous through our own efforts. They replaced this root and branch by an emphasis on grace and faith. Yet while righteousness was imputed through the merits of Christ alone, the Reformers maintained that the individual who was declared righteous by grace through faith must move toward internal moral transformation by that very same grace and faith. Luther taught that this happened through the believer's relationship with the Word and sacrament. Due to the primary place of the cross and forgiveness in his theology, his emphasis was on mortifying the flesh, the sin nature, rather than on living the resurrected life in God.[4] Calvin taught that sanctification was a continual work of the Spirit in the believer and that the Spirit will always make holiness a point of concern in the true believer.[5] The evidences of growing holiness are not works of the believer so much as God-given virtues.[6]

The Lutheran Formula of Concord says this:

> As soon as the Holy Ghost ... has begun in us this work of regeneration and renewal (sanctification) it is certain that through the power of the Holy Ghost we can and should co-operate ... from the new powers and gifts which the Holy Ghost has begun in us at conversion.[7]

The seventeenth-century Puritan John Owen reflected more deeply than perhaps any other theologian I know on the matter of sanctification. As we noted earlier, he defined it as

> a virtue, a power, a principle of the spiritual life and grace, wrought, created, infused into our souls, antecedent to and the next cause of true acts of holiness.[8]

Owen stressed that God was the author of sanctification, which the Spirit was carrying through the regeneration he had already worked in the elect. Holiness was a habit infused in the mind, will, and affections of the believer, making actual an obedience to God's commandments and conformity to the likeness of Christ. The Holy Spirit is the procuring cause of purity, he said, through the application of "Jesus' ever warm blood" as efficient cause.[9] Sanctification is a principle wrought and preserved by the Spirit, but one where the believer has a responsibility to mortify sin, have godly sorrow at sin, daily cleanse the heart and mind, and commune with God. Good works—obedience to the laws of God and the holy habits that mark the sanctified—do not stem from the individual but from the internal supernatural principle of grace. The new heart and new life given by the Spirit promised in Ezekiel 11 will cause the believer to obey God's statutes, not as law but as inevitable inclination.[10]

In 1692, Walter Marshall wrote one of the most widely distributed of all Puritan tracts, *The Gospel Mystery of Sanctification.* Attacking works righteousness, Marshall presented fourteen "directions" toward the sanctification of the believer, which he saw as

> no dream but a day to day evidence that the saints
> go from faith to faith as they grow in grace and in
> the knowledge of the Lord Jesus.

His thoroughgoing thesis argued that the holiness God requires is a holiness God provides. His third principle states, "There is no sanctification without the Holy Spirit." The Spirit unites us to Christ as the solitary and altogether sufficient fountain of spiritual life.

As a consequence, the believer is rooted and built up in the Spirit, and Christ is formed in him. Marshall rightly called this "a most bounteous gift of divine love." It is not the reestablishing of the old Adamic nature, which is to be mortified, but nothing less than the imaging of Christ in us. Sanctification is an internal grace, though Marshall reminds us that it is strengthened by God's provision of external means—he lists prayer, God's Word (read and preached), the sacraments, fellowship, psalm singing, and self-examination. These all foster union with Christ and nurture his image in us. By the encouragement and assurance of God's saving love, we are compelled to love God's law and desire his holiness.[11]

Pietism was a European movement that reacted to what it saw as the hard dogmatic theology of Lutheranism, seeking a more practical Christianity rooted in an intimate and warm experience and expression of the faith. It was a religion of the heart and affections. Pietists saw sanctification as a work of the Spirit through our responding obediently to the divine will revealed through the internal leadings of the Spirit, a kind of by-product of their spirituality of intimacy with Christ. Consequently they promoted the personal devotional life—coming near to the Savior, listening to his Word, faithfully cohering with that Word. Sadly, in the eighteenth and nineteenth centuries, holiness became their preoccupation rather than the by-product of intimacy with Christ; and this led to separation, isolation, and legalism. In this, some commentators see the road to a new justification by works.

The great eighteenth-century academic and revivalist Jonathan Edwards emphasized the role of the affections, which, when oriented to God in devotion, transform our character:

> Sanctification is the beauty of the Holy Spirit becoming the perfecting beauty of our humanity too, which is created to be indwelt by the Holy Spirit. The Holy Spirit, as Divine Love, activates our Holy Affections of love to God, without which we are incomplete.[12]

The modern Catholic scholar Brian Gaybba says it's not so much our love for God but the experience of God's love for us that transforms us:

> By sharing in the community and unity of God, we share in his holiness. The change in our lives does not take place all at once—like life itself it grows.... Love changes us at the depth of our being. Good works are the fruit, expressing the presence of love.[13]

In the eighteenth century, as we have seen, John Wesley's *The Plain Account of Christian Perfection* was taken up by the Methodists and subsequent nineteenth-century holiness movements, who taught that the believer could attain—and should pray for and pursue—entire sanctification, with freedom from all known sin. They often spoke of it as the experience of being "perfected in love." It was generally taught that this was a definite "experience," a gift of grace by the Spirit subsequent to conversion. Though considered a gift, this thesis led to striving, and yet another road to works righteousness was paved! The influential American evangelist Charles Finney also taught this, calling it "perfect love" or "entire sanctification."

At the end of their lives, John and Charles Wesley admitted in correspondence that, while they had taught this doctrine faithfully, they had seen no real evidence of it working! In a letter to Miss Jane Hilton many years into their ministry, John admitted:

> Although many taste of the heavenly gift, deliverance from inbred sin, yet so few, so exceedingly few, retain it one year, hardly one in ten, nay one in thirty.[14]

Hardly one in thirty showed evidence of entire sanctification a year after having claimed an experience of the Spirit. And more than that, John Wesley wrote to Dr. William Dodd about his own failure to live up to his message of entire perfection:

> I tell you flat, I have not attained the character I draw.[15]

J. Sidlow Baxter pointedly noted that, by the end of his ministry when he was struck by the lack of any real evidence for entire perfection, Wesley's doctrine of a one-off experience that ended sin had been so trimmed as to be "a self-contradictory concept of imperfect perfection."[16]

This endowment of the Spirit for perfection morphed in the nineteenth-century American holiness movement into the pursuit for the baptism of the Spirit (which later influenced the twentieth-century Pentecostal movement). No longer an experience that gave victory over sin, Spirit baptism was now seen as an experience of power for ministry. Some within the Pentecostal tradition would still argue that personal holiness is the necessary precondition for the baptism of power, but I can't help thinking of King Saul or even the Corinthians, who welcomed the Spirit for his charisms but rejected the Spirit for his character.

In the Reformed tradition, sanctification has generally been defined in terms of likeness to Christ. We have already noted that Louis Berkhof wrote of

> that gracious and continuous operation of the Holy Spirit by which He delivers the justified sinner from the pollution of sin, renews his whole nature in the image of God, and enables him to perform good works.[17]

Millard Erickson defined sanctification in relation to Christ as

> the Spirit at work in the believer bringing about the likeness of Christ.[18]

So what can we learn from our brief synopsis of church historical reflection on sanctification? Personally, I am encouraged that they all think holiness is not pie in the sky but a progressive, realizable goal. With the exception of the Wesleyan perfectionists—and even they admit that their one-off experience needs maintaining—the majority presuppose a process and a progress. They all emphasize the central role of the Holy Spirit in making me holy. Many emphasize my responsibility to partner with the Spirit—through obedience but not striving, being responsive to his leadings, spending time in devotion, and receiving the means of grace. Several emphasize that love is at the center—not dutiful obedience to law but transformation through my loving God and being loved by God. The goal is likeness to Christ—the Holy Spirit not only glorifies the Son but makes us like him.

THE SPIRIT HELPS US LOVE GOD

It seems to me that the Catholic scholar Brian Gaybba; the last great Puritan, Jonathan Edwards; and the Methodist revivalist John Wesley—although they were all different in nuance—were on to something really important. For them holiness was understood in terms of love. It is the "perfection of love"—the fruit of God's love for me and my love for God. Whether through pursuing God for an experience of his Spirit (Wesley) or through growing steadily living in the divine community of love (Gaybba) or through focusing our affections on God (Edwards), in every case a greater experience of divine love brings a greater measure of divine holiness.

Jesus explicitly linked together love for God, obedience to commandments, and the Holy Spirit: "If you love me, you will keep my commandments. And I will ask the Father, and he will give you another Helper, to be with you forever, even the Spirit" (John 14:15–17 ESV). He didn't mean that the Spirit is to be seen as a reward for keeping his commandments—the Spirit is the means to keep the commandments. Loving God cannot be mustered up; it is not the basis to receive the Spirit. It is not a work; it is an outworking of God's love poured into us. We love him who loved us (1 John 4:10, 19); we love as we receive his love poured into us (Rom. 5:5).

As we love God and our neighbor, we fulfill the law, the statutes of righteousness. We are holy.

Holiness is a love child. It is the fruit of the Spirit of love living in us. That love is his affection for us, and the love we experience becomes the love we express as we love God in return. To be filled with God as love is to cause us to love not only God but our neighbor. And this loving of God and neighbor fulfills the law. Augustine rightly said, "Love God and do what you want"—for if we truly love God, what we want will be what he wants, and that will fulfill all righteousness.

If we think of holiness in terms of duty, regulation, obligation, and rule, we miss the point, and we tend toward a legalism that brings pride or condemnation. Holiness can then appear harsh, and we resent it. But if we rightly understand holiness as a consequence of love lived out, an expression of affection for God, then we will come to value it all the more. Holiness: effect, not cause. Holiness: loving God. Loving God is the effect of knowing that God loves us. So if we are to be more holy, we must apply ourselves to knowing and showing more of God's love.

We are to love God with all our heart, soul, and strength. In the midst of a list of commandments given through Moses, we find this one, which Jesus reiterated as the greatest of all (Matt. 22:37–38), qualifying it with a second commandment to love our neighbors as ourselves. Jesus said that all the laws given and all the prophets' words may be summed up in these two commands. Holiness is completed in loving God with all we have and loving our neighbor as we love ourselves. If we would fulfill all the law, if we would express all holiness, then we must learn to live in love—we must bring all our being into line with the Spirit of love, who is the God of love, who causes us to love.

We are to apply these three—heart, soul, and strength—to loving God, to holiness. And we can see these three categories used later by Paul, as he connects them to life in the Spirit, bringing about holy living:

- **Heart** relates to our affections, loving, devoting—*the holy heart:* 2 Cor. 3:17–18.
- **Soul** relates to our mind, intellect, will—*the holy mind:* Rom. 8:4–9.
- **Strength** relates to our body, doing, acting—*the holy body:* Gal. 5:16–25.

1. The Spirit and the heart

Now the Lord is the Spirit, and where the Spirit of the Lord is, there is freedom. And we all, with unveiled face, beholding the glory of the Lord, are being transformed into the same image from one degree of glory to another. For this comes from the Lord who is the Spirit. (2 Cor. 3:17–18 ESV)

Moses knew God face-to-face, as a man speaks with a friend (Ex. 33:11). His encounter with God knew no obstacle, except that exposure which God withheld so as not to consume him (Ex. 33:22–23). As a face exposed to the sun glows with its heat, so Moses' face glowed with divine glory. When he descended to the Israelite camp, he would cover his face with a veil because the people were too afraid to come near him, as if that diminishing residue of God's glory might consume them (Ex. 34:30–35). Something of God was left with Moses after their meetings, though just like our suntans, the glory would inevitably fade.

Paul used this as an analogy to show an amazing truth about our relationship to God through Christ, by the Spirit. Whereas God's people, the Jews, have a face veiled to God, a heart closed, Christians have a face unveiled to God, a heart open. A veil is a symbol of protection, discretion, covering. But we by the Spirit have liberty from fear and condemnation, and this means we may draw near. We by the Spirit may behold Christ, God's glory incarnate. Whereas Moses knew a fading glory after departing from God's presence, we may know an increase of glory, for we never need leave God's presence. It's remarkable—Moses looked at God, but by the Spirit we may look like God!

In the ancient Near East, the veil, of course, was worn only by women, to keep their beauty, their intimacy, from all save their husband. The veil was removed only on the wedding night when the wife was fully known by her beloved. There is surely more than a hint here that there exists no veil between us and God but rather a profound knowing by the Spirit. We are to have a communion and a consummation, whereby God's name is not merely given to us, but his very image is imprinted on us.

As we gaze on his glory, without hindrance, impediment, or fear, as our face and heart turn toward Jesus, the Spirit does not simply allow that glory to rest superficially on our faces as on Moses; he does a deep work of transformation, turning us into the very image of that which we behold. It is clearly not an instantaneous transformation—and Paul's verb certainly suggests a process, not a completed event—but there is a sense of intensifying the image of Christ in us. The Spirit always points us to Christ, and he always makes us like the Christ he points us to. Of course, we can resist. We can choose to lose ourselves, to give ourselves to other things, even legitimate ones. What we give ourselves to molds us. What we continually look at, we begin to look like. Just as those who give their attention to violent films can become violent, so those who give themselves to things of beauty are beautified.

Christ is sinless, and as we allow ourselves to be led by the Spirit, something of that sinless nature rubs off on us. As we devote ourselves to Jesus, constantly looking to him, meditating on his sublime words, his sinless life, his grace-filled acts, his agonizing substitutionary death, his victorious resurrection, his glorious ascension, his majestic reign, his anticipated glory, his unassailable power, his matchless beauty, his breathtaking wisdom—oh, as we look face-to-face with Jesus, so we are transformed, perfected, like a caterpillar changed into a butterfly. But we must make time to meditate on Christ and allow the Spirit to mold us into his likeness.

2. The Spirit and the mind (soul)

> *... in order that the righteous requirements of the law might be fully met in us, who do not live according to the sinful nature but according to the Spirit. Those who live according to the sinful nature have their minds set on what that nature desires; but those who*

live in accordance with the Spirit have their minds set on what the Spirit desires. The mind of sinful man is death, but the mind controlled by the Spirit is life and peace; the sinful mind is hostile to God. It does not submit to God's law, nor can it do so. Those controlled by the sinful nature cannot please God. You, however, are controlled not by the sinful nature but by the Spirit, if the Spirit of God lives in you. (Rom. 8:4–9)

Paul wrote that we are to walk by the Spirit—we are to live by the Spirit and so be able to fully meet the righteous demands of the law. That is holiness. By dying for us fully, Christ satisfied the demands of the law and our due punishment for failing the law. However, now, by the Spirit, we can fulfill the law. Paul contrasted a Spirit-led life, fulfilling the requirements of the law, with the opposite way of life, "walking according to the flesh."

The mind is a battlefield—whoever controls the mind controls the person. Paul assumed that the Christian who has the Holy Spirit will let the Spirit have them. The command center, the control, is the mind:

- The spiritual man has his mind on things that God desires.
- The natural man has his mind on things the flesh craves.
- The spiritual man has a mind that brings life and peace.
- The natural man has a mind that brings death.
- The spiritual man has a mind that lives to please God and submit to his law.

- The natural man has a mind hostile to God that rejects God's law.
- The spiritual man's mind is filled with the things of the Spirit.
- The natural man's mind is filled with the things of this world.

The fallen sinful human nature is manifest in a mind that is directed toward things of this world—its values, its measures, its pleasures. The fallen sinful human nature will want to direct a life to fall in line with a world that is hostile to God and whose prince is Satan. The mind is a window into the person—it reveals who each of us is. The mind is like a rudder; it directs the course we take. We have a responsibility to give our minds over to the Spirit to direct our thinking, which in turn shapes our acting. The Spirit-led mind will lead us to a law-fulfilling, God-honoring, holy life.

Paul said later in Romans, "Do not be conformed to this world, but be transformed by the renewal of your mind, that by testing you may discern what is the will of God, what is good and acceptable and perfect" (Rom. 12:2 ESV). Transformation of the life occurs through "nonconforming" to the world, by a renewal of our mind in accord with God's revealed will of what is perfect. Therefore, we need to self-consciously and actively "set [our] minds on things above [where Christ is seated], not on earthly things" (Col. 3:2). We must fill our minds with that which is good and acceptable and perfect in God's sight. What do I spend most of my time thinking about, watching, feeding on, reading? What images imprint themselves on my mind? What am I programming my mind with? Is it a mind ordered by

God's truth, set out in Scripture, a mind that thinks on that which is "true … honorable … just … pure … lovely … commendable … excellen[t] … worthy of praise" (Phil. 4:8 ESV)?

3. The Spirit and the body (strength)

> *So I say, live by the Spirit, and you will not gratify the desires of the sinful nature. For the sinful nature desires what is contrary to the Spirit, and the Spirit what is contrary to the sinful nature. They are in conflict with each other, so that you do not do what you want. But if you are led by the Spirit, you are not under law. The acts of the sinful nature are obvious: sexual immorality, impurity and debauchery; idolatry and witchcraft; hatred, discord, jealousy, fits of rage, selfish ambition, dissensions, factions and envy; drunkenness, orgies, and the like. I warn you, as I did before, that those who live like this will not inherit the kingdom of God. But the fruit of the Spirit is love, joy, peace, patience, kindness, goodness, faithfulness, gentleness and self-control. Against such things there is no law. Those who belong to Christ Jesus have crucified the sinful nature with its passions and desires. Since we live by the Spirit, let us keep in step with the Spirit. (Gal. 5:16–25)*

The sinful nature desires what is contrary to the Spirit. That sinful nature, still operative in our flesh, wages war against the Spirit, who dwells with our spirit. There is no hint in the Bible that the Christian is free from struggle once saved. On the contrary, the struggle may intensify.

Paul informed the Galatian Christians of this because their law-keeping efforts were clearly powerless to keep the flesh at bay. Paul presented them with a choice—to walk in the Spirit and bear his fruit, or to walk in the flesh. He laid the blame on neither the Devil nor the flesh but rather on the individual's choosing to follow them! We clearly have a choice in how we will live—the power of the Spirit is readily available to help us as we make the right choice.

The fifteen listed sins of the flesh are not exhaustive but illustrative. They cover four categories: sexual sins, religious deviation, relational disorder, and signs of intemperance.[19] This extensive list of sins (verses 19–21) may seem to be out of place in a letter addressed to Christians. But sadly, those familiar with the church will know better. In fact, in a church where the law is heavily laid down and where the Holy Spirit is not honored to help, the law almost fuels the flesh, and manifest sins result. My own experience is that in those churches that refuse to rely on the Spirit but heavily lay down laws—and whose religion is one of prohibition—the flesh is manifest in all the sexual sins and sins of dissension, division, anger, etc., that Paul highlighted. But where the Spirit of the Lord is allowed to lead, there is liberty.

Paul was very clear-cut: If our lives are led by the Spirit and we spend our lives in the milieu of the Spirit, keeping in step with the Spirit's directing, we won't gratify the sinful nature. And if we are led by the Spirit, we are not under the Old Testament Law—a law that is powerless to help and can only condemn. We are, however, under the covenant of grace, where there is both "no condemnation" (Rom. 8:1) and true conformation to the law by the Spirit.

When we walk in the Spirit, we bear fruit. Fruit is not a reward, it is not an effort, it is not a work, and we do not muster it up. As fruit grows naturally on trees, so spiritual fruit grows naturally on Spirit-led Christians. Love, joy, peace, patience, kindness, goodness, faithfulness, gentleness, self-control—these are the fruits the Spirit grows; these are the facets of Christ's character imprinted on our lives. Before these, the law of God, which cannot produce fruit but only point out sin, stands silent but approving.

To be led by the Spirit into bearing fruit, rather than to be led by the sinful nature into works of the flesh, requires being attentive and obedient. There is nothing passive about it—no being "caught up. It is a presupposed tenacity to conformity to God's will. R. Y. K. Fung said walking in the Spirit "is to be under the constant, moment-by-moment direction, control, and guidance of the Spirit."[20] We must not do what comes naturally—that is, according to our flesh nature; we must do what comes supernaturally, living to please God and doing only that for which he gives permission and which brings him pleasure. The list of imperatives Paul gave makes it clear, yet again, that we must take responsibility to live spiritually. And over all there is hope—this is not an unattainable list of virtues to which we aspire; holiness, defined in terms of fruit, will be evident if we will be led by the Spirit.

Paul concluded by reminding us that "those who belong to Christ Jesus have crucified the sinful nature with its passions and desires" (Gal. 5:24). This is in the aorist tense, which means it refers to a completed, one-off event. F. F. Bruce rightly said that it is the cross of Christ that makes this clean break with the past, a past of sin and condemnation by the law.[21] As we saw in our exploration of Romans 6, it is this union with Christ, this cocrucifixion and coresurrection, that is the power base for our life led free of sin in the power of the Spirit. It is from this judicial place of freedom from the curse of the law, and this actual place of being "a new creation in Christ," that we may freely keep in step with the Spirit—free not to indulge in the impulses of the flesh but to produce the fruits of holiness.

Chapter 11
Staying Holy

*No one who abides in him keeps on sinning. (1 John
3:6 ESV)*

As we have looked at the practicalities of a holy life, we have considered what it is to die to sin, and we have explored how we may walk in the Spirit. But how are we to keep going? Our third principle for holy living is to *abide in Christ*. It is a glorious concept, defining the very heart and the means to live a holy and victorious Christian life.

ABIDE IN ME

We often sing the famous hymn "Abide with Me," especially at funerals. In fact, as Christians we do not so much need to ask God to abide with us—he has promised already never to leave us or forsake us—as to obey his injunction to abide in him. And he promises us that, if we do, benefits will come to us. And so John made this startling statement: "No one who abides in [Jesus] keeps on sinning" (1 John 3:6 ESV).

This text has led some to feel condemned as they continue in sin. Others feel confused, as John elsewhere seems to suggest that ongoing sin is most certainly an issue, such that forgiveness was provided for (1 John 1:8–10). But I suspect John's intention is as much pastoral as theological. It is a statement of *hope* and of *how*—the hope that we can in truth be free of sin, and the how of abiding in him. John set this statement in context by saying that the very reason Jesus appeared was to take away our sin, adding that there is no sin in him (1 John 3:5). John concluded that, to the extent that we abide in the sinless one, the sin remover, we will be sinless. Bishop Stephen Smalley summed up:

> If the purpose of Christ appearing was "to abolish sins," and his eternal nature is sinless, it follows that the person who "lives in him" ... should be similarly without sin.[1]

John did not want to condemn; he wanted to encourage, reminding us that we need not be victims of sin. New Testament scholar John Christopher Thomas said this statement is "staggering" because of its optimism regarding believers' ability not to sin—while recognizing the believers' reality of sinning.[2]

The parent who reacts with outbursts of temper at the children can be gentle and patient; the man addicted to pornography can be clean; the person absorbed in self-pity and constantly craving other people's affirmation can be secure; the boss who makes his colleagues' lives a misery by control and abuse can become kind; the consumer who buys and buys, just to impress others, can be content; the arrogant and condescending can walk humbly; the vulgar-minded and vulgar-mouthed can be made pure. Sin that clings can be cleared away—and patterns of sin, programs of addiction, can be broken. How? By abiding in Christ rather than abiding in sin.

A friend told me he was counseling a young man struggling with masturbation. My pal wisely and simply said, "Practice the presence of God, not the presence of lust." Many abide in sin. The addict to porn often abides at his computer screen. The greedy consumer abides in magazines or shop windows. The self-pitying abide in painful memories. The arrogant and proud abide in their achievements. As Christians, we are meant to live and move and have our being in Christ—yet for many of us who stay strangled by sin, we live and move and have our being in our sin.

WHERE DO YOU LIVE?

What is often needed is not more ministry, counseling, deliverance, or inner healing. I am grateful for these provisions in the church—yet I have seen people time and time and time again come to the front of church, confess their sin, and receive prayer ministry, only to return to their sin on Monday and then return to the front next Sunday for more of the same. The cycle of sin-confession-prayer, sin-confession-prayer can cease. Freedom can come. There is genuine hope of genuine holiness. And the key is to abide in Christ. Many Christians are still in their sin because they abide in sin. They visit Christ, but they live in sin. Pentecostal father A. T. Pierson once rightly noted:

All practical power over sin and over men depends on maintaining closest communion. Those who abide in the secret place with God show themselves mighty to conquer evil and strong to work and to war for God.

When John wrote that "anyone who abides in Jesus will not [continue in] sin," the term he used for *sin* was a present participle, meaning "habitually keep on sinning." So this is not a reference to a state of sinless perfection but an ongoing process—as we abide, Christ reveals more sin in our nature that he needs to remove. Nevertheless, it gives hope that revealed sin can be removed sin. The more we abide in Christ, the more we become aware of our sin and joined to that power source to transform us. Charles Simeon, the famous Cambridge minister, called this "habitual nearness to God." Sadly, the reality is that many live in habitual nearness to sin. Like Lot's wife, many people constantly look back to the city of sin under judgment rather than dwell in fellowship and obedience with the three divine visitors.

So we must face up to the challenge: Where are we abiding? In Christ or in sin?

WHAT DOES IT MEAN TO ABIDE?

The term *abide* is a favored term of John's and is found repeatedly on Christ's lips in John 15 and throughout 1 John. Of the 120 occurrences in the New Testament, 69 are found in John's literature—40 in John's gospel alone. The Greek word is a primary verb, *meno*, and is represented in translation by this range of words: "abide, remain,

stay, live, dwell, lodge, continue, last, persist, await, wait."[3] In its
noun form, it depicts an abode—a room or a dwelling. The English
verb that generally is used to translate *meno* is *abide* and is related to
the noun *abode*.

To abide is to live somewhere—not to lodge, not to visit, but to
dwell, to be a resident. The one who abides is the one who does not
leave the sphere or realm in which they find themselves. They remain
permanently. As a fish abides in water, because to leave would be to
die, so we are called to abide in Christ.

Jesus' imperative "abide in me" is also the greatest invitation—
even as the Father abides in Christ and Christ in the Father, so we
are invited to take up royal residence in God (John 14:10). This is
mind-blowing. We are called to live in God (1 John 4:12–16). Adam
lived in the garden and walked with God, who visited him daily in
the cool of the day; we live in God, in permanent proximity and
intimacy.

Imagine the Queen of England requesting that you come and
take rooms in Buckingham Palace or Windsor Castle and join her
family—a privilege I doubt any have ever been afforded who weren't
relations or servants or dogs. But how much greater is the invitation
to come and live in Christ, to abide in him!

WELCOME HOME

Jesus began his discourse in John 15 employing the analogy of a vine
with its branches. He is the vine, and we are the branches; as we
abide, we bear fruit.

By saying he is the true vine (v. 1), he was saying there are other
vines that are false—wild vines, rogue vines, pretend vines. The vine

was a symbol frequently used to describe Israel in the Old Testament, normally in negative terms of being fruitless and faithless and the object of punishment (Hos. 10:1; Isa. 5:1; Jer. 2:21; Ps. 80:8–16). On the coins of the intertestamental Maccabean period, Israel was depicted as a vine; the gates to Herod's temple portrayed a sculpted vine and the temple facade, and entrance doors were golden vines with hanging clusters as tall as a person.[4]

When Jesus declared himself as the true vine, he was saying that in himself he represents the fulfillment of all that Israel represented—he is the new true Israel of God; he is the living temple of God. Only by being in him can anyone seek to bear fruit. Jesus said that God the Father is a gardener who cuts off all fruitless branches. This has caused some to fear that God will throw away fruitless believers, or apostate Christians, into eternal damnation. But that was not Jesus' point—he made it very clear here and elsewhere that there is security in him. The disciples were already clean because of the gospel Christ had delivered and they received (John 15:3). It is likely the unfruitful branch refers to those Jews who rejected Christ, who refused to live in him: These branches will be thrown away (Rom. 11:17).[5] Jesus is the true vine, and fruitfulness comes only through abiding in him—not through the Jew continuing in his Judaism detached from Jesus.

Fruitfulness is the fruit of righteousness; it is holiness, and it comes only through being grafted into Christ, only by having his life flowing through us. Branches cannot bear fruit if they are not connected to the vine. The Jew cannot bear fruit if he is not connected to the true vine. A Christian can only bear fruit if he is abiding in the vine.

Branches must stay connected to the vine; Jesus then said repeatedly "abide in me" (five times in John 15:4–7). Live a life connected to Christ. Live in him. Live without separation from him. Live with all his life flowing through you—you in him and he in you. Abiding in Jesus is not a hard place. Christ is love, so to abide in Christ is to abide in his love (vv. 9–10). It is to accept the embrace of grace. It is not an abiding in law but an abiding in love; not an abiding in obligation but an abiding in affection. It is willingness to be loved by Jesus and to love him.

How many believe they are abiding in Jesus when in fact they are abiding in religion? They abide in their denominations, church traditions, confessions, and creeds. They abide in the teachings and liturgies and sacraments of their religious fathers. These have their place, but only to frame the vine in which we abide. Abiding in religion can easily become a substitute for abiding in Christ. The Pharisees abided in religion. The medieval Catholic Church abided in religion. The Reformed church can so easily abide in Calvin. The Brethren church abided in separation from the world. The heavy shepherding of the charismatic movement abided under control. The liberal church has made a virtue of abiding in the world. The pietistic tradition made a virtue out of abiding in their devotions. The place of abiding is Jesus Christ; the proof of abiding is holiness and fruitfulness.

We must constantly examine our Christian life and ask where we are abiding. From where are we drawing our spiritual life? To what are we being fashioned and formed? Is Jesus the source and goal, the daily diet—is his fragrance, his beauty, his word in everything we do?

Bishop J. C. Ryle, the famous teacher on holiness, described it like this:

> "Abide in me," says Jesus. Cling to me. Stick fast to me. Live the life of close and intimate communion with me. Get nearer to me. Roll every burden on me. Cast your whole weight on me. Never let go your hold on me for a moment. Be, as it were, rooted and planted in me. Do this and I will never fail you. I will ever abide in you.[6]

HOW DO WE ABIDE?

You cannot dwell in two or more places at the same time. You cannot abide in Jesus and in religion or yourself or the world. Andrew Murray, the Keswick father who exhorted the church to live the victorious life, said,

> Abide in Jesus the sinless one—which means give up all of self and its life and dwell in God's will and rest in his strength. That is what brings the power that does not commit sin.[7]

In a similar vein, the nineteenth-century American revivalist Charles Finney said,

> Being in Christ implies that we are out of ourselves, in the sense in which selfish men are in themselves....The selfish man lives to himself. Self is the

precise end for which he lives, labors, plans and cares. Hence, concisely speaking, he is in himself. But to be in Christ, he must cease to live and to be in himself, and must in some sense, come to be and to live in Christ…. To commit yourself to Christ, implies that you merge yourself in him—make him your end of life—make his glory your supreme end in all you do.[8]

1. Recognize his lordship.

John tells us, "Whoever confesses that Jesus is the Son of God, God abides in him" (1 John 4:15 ESV). The moment we recognize and receive Jesus as Lord, as God's Son and our Savior, we are joined to him, and we abide in him. While that initial moment of commitment and incorporation cannot be repeated, it needs daily to be ratified.

When Jesus said "abide in me," he used an aorist imperative, which translates literally as "begin to remain in me." Its tense suggests a past event with a present effect—a starting point, as we enter into mutual indwelling.[9] And so the word also implies continuity. To abide in Christ is to remain in him moment by moment, daily, weekly, monthly, as we renew our allegiance to Jesus and avow to live in him and have him live through us.

2. Identify and participate in his death.

Jesus said, "Whoever eats my flesh and drinks my blood remains in me, and I in him" (John 6:56). Many interpret this in a sacramental manner, applying it to the regular receiving of Holy

Communion (the Lord's Supper). Clearly, that is not far from the thought here, but Communion remains symbolic of the deeper reception of Christ in his saving work. There are many who have received Communion and certainly did not abide in Christ—one merely thinks of Stalin or Hitler to prove the point. Holy Communion symbolizes and sacramentally administers the grace of God poured out at Calvary when Christ's body was crushed against a tree and his precious life poured out. Those who believe and receive this are those who spiritually eat and drink and are united with Christ.

3. Commit to continual prayer.

"If you remain in me and my words remain in you, ask whatever you wish, and it will be given you" (John 15:7). In speaking of abiding, Jesus mentioned prevailing prayer. It is in prayer that we listen to, learn from, love, and are led by God. Prayer is the language of intimacy. Prayer keeps communion. And prayer bears fruit, not simply in answered prayer, but in presenting us to a holy God to be transformed into his likeness. The master teacher and writer on prayer E. M. Bounds wrote,

> The first and last stages of holy living are crowned with praying.[10]

The renowned Puritan John Bunyan said,

> Prayer will make a man cease from sin, or sin will entice a man to cease from prayer.[11]

A simple and revealing question to ask anyone gripped by sin but looking for pastoral help is, "Tell me about your prayer life." To pray is to place oneself before God and under God—to pray is to avail oneself of God's power. If someone repeatedly comes to you asking for your prayers for help to not sin or to bear fruit, and if it transpires that person is not praying as well, you might do more by sending him or her away with the words, "Why don't you pray for you, and then I'll pray for you? Pray for yourself first, and then I'll join you."

4. Undertake a studied obedience to God's Word.

Jesus said, "If you obey my commands, you will remain in my love" (John 15:10). John wrote, "If what you heard from the beginning abides in you, then you too will abide in the Son and in the Father.... Whoever keeps his commandments abides in God, and God in him" (1 John 2:24; 3:24 ESV). Scripture tells us what God requires of us and how we may fulfill it.

We noted John Bunyan's comment that prayer would keep a man from sin or sin would keep a man from prayer. In a similar vein, he wrote this inside the cover of his own Bible:

> This book will keep you from sin, or sin will keep
> you from this book.

Many years ago, a worship leader named David asked the question, "How can a young man keep his way pure?" ... and he revealed the key: "By living according to your word" (Ps. 119:9). If it is holiness we are after, then it is Scripture we must study. For in God's Word is revealed God's will for us and his way to that will. Again, some people seek to put on the pastor or counselor the responsibility for their holiness—getting someone else to pray for them, to study for them, to direct them. We should constantly be directing people to Scripture—to meet God personally there, to hear and heed him.

WHAT IF WE ABIDE?

While the simple fact of abiding in Christ is privilege and pleasure enough, nevertheless, there are several consequences of abiding. Most notable for our purposes is the fruit of holiness. But abiding in Christ, having his life flow through us, brings a whole host of delights.

1. There will be pruning.

We know that dead branches, those detached from Christ the vine, are thrown away. But even branches connected to Christ are pruned (John 15:2). God lovingly inspects his vine—with all the tenderness and attentiveness of a gardener with his prize plant. I never met a gardener who wasn't passionate about his plants, who didn't love them, care for them, and seek to bring out the best in them. And so it is with God. He is proud of us, and he prunes because he wants the best for us and from us. He is looking for much fruit, and so he prunes us to increase the crop. As he cuts away some of the flourishing leaves and some of the wild offshoots, the branch becomes stronger, and the nourishing life does not dissipate but creates a weightier fruit cluster.

Pruning makes a weak vine stronger. God prunes his church because he wants us to be the best we can be. He does not let us grow wild; he wants us to grow fruitful. The knife with which he prunes may well be storms and trials, disciplines and difficulties. But the goal is always our good. Many Christians resist pruning, preferring to grow in their own way. But that way, we fail to be all that God would have us be.

2. There will be much fruit.

Jesus spoke not simply of fruit but of "much fruit" (vv. 5, 8). What was the fruit Jesus was thinking of? I believe it can be understood in two ways: Christlike character and Christlike ministry. Vines grow grapes, not olives—the fruit of abiding in Christ will be to produce fruit after his DNA. We will resemble Christ. The fruits Paul depicts in Galatians 5:22–23 are all facets of Christ's character, and we can expect these to be seen in us.

But as well as fruit of character, there will be fruit in ministry. Jesus said that the one who believes in him will do what he did—indeed he will do "even greater things" (John 14:12). He is talking about miracles; and the one who believes is the one who abides, and the one who abides may expect to bear fruit of ministry, even into the miraculous. This fruit is lasting fruit (15:16)—it will not wither on the vine; it will not be enjoyed for a season only to have its memory pass. The fruit we bear will become the crowns we wear in eternity.

3. God will be glorified.

"This is to my Father's glory, that you bear much fruit" (v. 8). The famous statement of Reformed doctrine, the Westminster Shorter Catechism, states that the chief end of man is to glorify God and to enjoy him forever. We glorify God not simply by praising his glory but by living in such a way as to bring him glory. He receives glory when we abide and produce a fruitful life in Christlike character. He receives glory when we abide and enter an effective Christlike kingdom ministry—extending God's reign in people's lives, seeing the sick healed, setting the prisoners free, and proclaiming good news to the poor. The abiding life is one that magnifies God, a life so fruitful that God is credited with doing a great and marvelous work. But we must beware that the converse is true: If we seek glory for ourselves rather than for God, we will never abide in him.

4. Prayers will be answered.

"If you remain in me and my words remain in you, ask whatever you wish, and it will be given you" (v. 7). What a remarkable offer! Christ promises answers to prayers that are prayed from an abiding life.

Not every prayer request is granted. Why? Because some are not prayed from an abiding life. Many prayers come from self and not from God. The Christian who abides in Christ, who is in communion and intimacy with Christ, will know his will. In fact, the abiding Christian wills what God wills. Thus the prayer of the abiding believer is the heart echo of the One we are abiding in; so it is not surprising that the prayer is heard and answered. Many of us ask what God doesn't will, and so we don't get what we ask for.

5. Joy will be complete.

"I have told you this so that my joy may be in you and that your joy may be complete" (v. 11). C. S. Lewis once wrote that joy is "the serious business of Heaven."[12] Those who live in Christ live in the King of heaven. To abide in Jesus is to explode with joy. The joyless Christian is detached from Christ, whereas the abiding Christian will know fullness of joy, complete and replete. At times Christianity is depicted as dull, dry, and depressing, but that's when Christianity has been more about religion than remaining in Christ.

John Owen wrote:

> If we are satisfied with vague ideas about him we shall find no transforming power communicated to us. But when we cling wholeheartedly to him and our minds are filled with thoughts of him and we constantly delight ourselves in him, then spiritual power will flow from him to purify our hearts, increase our holiness, strengthen our graces, and sometimes fill us "with joy inexpressible and full of glory."[13]

6. Sin will diminish.

"No one who abides in him keeps on sinning.... Whoever says he abides in him ought to walk in the same way in which [Jesus] walked" (1 John 3:6; 2:6 ESV). Here we have both precept and promise. The precept: We are commanded to walk as Jesus walked, in holiness and fruitfulness of life, abiding in Christ. And the promise: If we abide in him, then we will walk as he walked. If we make Christ the grammar of our being—our whole existence *in, of, from, to, for, by, with,* and *through* him alone—then we shall live as he lived and no longer continue in sin.

GODLIKE

Abiding does not save us. Jesus said, "You are already clean because of the word I have spoken to you" (John 15:3). But abiding progressively sanctifies us. It is not our effort that bears fruit, for we cannot bear fruit by ourselves (v. 4). Fruit will grow only when the branch is connected to the healthy vine. But fruit will surely come as we stay in Christ. Jesus said, "Apart from me you can do nothing" (v. 5), and he meant it. We cannot make ourselves holy. Holiness comes as a gift and a by-product of abiding in Christ, his indwelling Spirit transforming us.

The extent of our holiness is dependent on the extent of our abiding. Do any of us ever really abide so deeply that we walk in perfect holiness as stated by John in 1 John 3:6? I have yet to meet anyone who does. But "let God be true, and every man a liar" (Rom. 3:4)—"his divine power has given us everything we need for life and godliness" (2 Peter 1:3). Let our goal be set not by those who have failed the standard and sinned but by the standard set by Jesus himself: being perfect as our heavenly Father is perfect. Being Godlike.

Chapter 12
When Holiness Spreads Like Fire

On the eve of Israel's entry into the Promised Land, Joshua said this to the people:

> *Consecrate yourselves, for tomorrow the LORD will do amazing things among you. (Josh. 3:5)*

I come from a tradition that longs for God to do amazing things among us—to stretch out his hand in power; to manifest his presence and his glory; to visit our churches, our community, and our society in such an unmissable manner that people will be filled with awe, amazing signs and wonders will be performed, the gospel will be heralded and heard with compelling conviction, and the Lord will add daily to our number those being saved. It is my sincere belief that the earliest days of the church in Jerusalem (Acts 2:43–47) need not be the most glorious.

And so, as I encountered this text in Joshua 3:5 one late autumn day in 2008, I was profoundly moved—was this the secret to the revival of the church that we longed for, prayed for, worked for? Was God calling me and my church to consecrate ourselves in order that a holy God might visit us and, in turn, bare his mighty arm through us?

If so, was I ready to consecrate myself? Did I even know what consecration looked like? Encouraged by my colleagues, I began the work that formed the basis for this book—to consider the nature of consecration and how we could be consecrated so that we might see the Lord do amazing things.

The study of holiness is not easy, for it exposes us to God's searching, searing word, before which we are laid bare. I confess at times I have wanted to give up on this study—for it pained me to see the gulf between God's laws and my life. Holiness is a doctrine that must be lived; it does not allow for the abstract. It may not be creedal, but it is certainly central to the Christian life.

CONSECRATION BRINGS VISITATION

Consecration, literally "setting apart as holy," creates the platform for divine visitation. Moses was first to command the people of Israel to consecrate themselves in preparation for God's manifestation. The word he used came from a word meaning "to cut" and involved abstaining from sexual relations and performing ritual washings (Ex. 19:22). Following their consecration, God's Spirit fell on seventy appointed leaders, who all prophesied. Then God drove quail in from the sea, enough to feed the million-plus nation of Israel tramping through the desert (Num. 11:18–33). Joshua then called the people of Israel to consecrate themselves in an outward act of obedience and pursuit of God. These "outward rites were meant to further inward openness toward God and his acts."[1]

On the day following their consecration, the Lord did amazing things—the whole nation crossed through the river Jordan "on dry ground," as the waters in full flood were held back by God's power (Josh. 3:13–17). Holiness makes way for God's manifest presence—his presence brings his demonstrated power.

This pattern is revealed in 2 Chronicles 5 when Solomon consecrated the new temple to God with worship and sacrifice. God came among them, and the glory of the Lord so filled the temple that the Levites could not continue work. Likewise, the time spent by the apostles and women in the upper room as they prayed following Christ's ascension were doubtless days of consecration, of setting apart their lives for God and allowing him to bring to light sins that they might confess. They set themselves apart, and then the Lord did amazing things among them at Pentecost when the fire of God fell. In Acts 19, a revival swept Ephesus through the apostolic ministry of Paul. The gospel truly influenced lives, and believers sought to consecrate themselves to the Lord, publicly confessing their sin (v. 18) and removing any trace of their sinful past, including burning all pagan and witchcraft material (v. 19). And after this consecration, the Lord did amazing things among them, closing down the idol-making industry as "the word of the Lord spread widely and grew in power" (v. 20).

Now, let it be said clearly that holiness is not merely some pragmatic response of ours to get God to do something exciting. Holiness, consecrating ourselves to God and to righteousness, is always God's word to us; and if only we were constantly complying with this, we would constantly be experiencing more of God. Holiness is an end in itself. Holiness is command and blessing. Regardless of its consequence, we consecrate out of obedience. As the Puritan Thomas Brookes said, "Holiness is its own reward." And yet holiness, though an end in itself, doesn't end there; holiness welcomes the Holy One, and the Holy One comes with all his glory and majesty and authority.

REVIVING HOLINESS IN THE CHURCH

The church wrongly expects people in the world to consecrate themselves to God, all too often rebuking the world for her sinfulness. As the nineteenth-century theologian John Henry Newman famously observed, "Every organization seems to start with a prophet and end with a policeman." Regrettably, as we considered at the outset of our exploration of holiness, the church today seems to prefer the role of policeman—pointing out and pointing at sin. And her message often sounds hollow because she herself is not holy. The church is called to be salt and light, not judge and jury. It is we who are to be so consecrated to God that God's presence in us permeates and changes the moral climate. Change must start with the church—the salt and light must be salty and shining before the church is of benefit to the world.

It is time for judgment to begin at the house of the Lord. God's Old Testament prophets almost always addressed their words first and foremost to God's people. Jesus didn't initially come to the Gentiles but came first to the sons of Israel, entering and cleaning out the temple long before the command to go clean out the nations was given. God's economy has always been to revive the church before she can reform the world. The great twentieth-century prophetic statesman Jim Wallis has said,

> The social transformation of the world alleviating poverty and disease, restoring human rights and religious freedom, bringing peace, overcoming prejudice, can only come through spiritual revival.[2]

Social transformation always follows spiritual renewal—never vice versa. That great student of revivals J. Edwin Orr noted that "revival effects [i.e., causes] churches," producing deep repentance and a greater holiness that brings a new release of power in witness and evangelism.[3] Revival begins in churches, and it begins with a passion for holiness. The father of the American awakening, Jonathan Edwards, wrote of his passion for holiness, a passion that was caught by the church and blazed through society:

> My longings after God and holiness were much increased. Pure and humble, holy and heavenly, Christianity appeared exceedingly amiable to me. I felt a burning desire to be, in every thing, a complete Christian; and conformed to the blessed image of Christ; and that I might live, in all things, according to the pure, sweet, and blessed rules of the gospel. I had an eager thirsting after progress in these things; which put me upon pursuing and pressing after them. It was my continual strife, day

and night, and constant inquiry, how I should be more holy, and live more holily, and more becoming a child of God, and a disciple of Christ.[4]

"Consecrate yourselves, for tomorrow I will do amazing things among you," says the Lord. Edwards did, and God came.

Canadian spiritual writer Henry Blackaby has said that God's people can shape a nation if they are holy. He offered these challenging words that should cause all leaders like me to truly search themselves:

> I believe there will be no revival [in society] without holiness in the leadership. None. Cry unto God all you want. He will not hear you. Pull together all the phrases that revivalists of other generations have all quoted, and it will not make an ounce of difference to the heart of God. God is looking for holiness![5]

Brian Edwards, in his study on revival, also singled out holiness in leaders as the make-or-break of revival:

> Without doubt unholiness by our Christian leaders is a major reason why we have so little spiritual success today.[6]

This is a point labored by E. M. Bounds in his classic work *Power Through Prayer*. He stated:

> It is not great talents or great learning or great preachers that God needs, but men [and women] great in faith, great in courage, great for God. Men [and women] always preaching by holy sermons in the pulpit, by holy lives outside it. These can mold a generation for God.[7]

In a letter to his father in 1734, John Wesley wrote, "My one aim in life is to secure personal holiness, for without being holy myself, I cannot promote real holiness in others." And we do well to remember that Wesley's own personal pursuit of holiness influenced a group of like-minded leaders who in turn established a church movement that shook a nation. The world really has seen what God can do through one man fully consecrated to him.[8] Again, Brian Edwards rightly said,

> Without exception those whom God uses in revival are men and women who fear God and sin and nothing else. They take seriously the command, 'Be holy as I am holy,' says the Lord.[9]

Sadly, after over twenty years in ministry and leadership, I have seen the church pursue just about everything but holiness: outreach programs; beginners' courses; marriage courses; discipleship programs; courses on spiritual gifts; church planting; fresh expressions; inner healing and deliverance courses; building reordering; endless conferences; worship conferences; communications seminars; workshops on multimedia use; religionless Christianity, then postmodern sacramentalizing Christianity; raves in the nave; rock mass; Taizé chanting … and I for one have tried them all! They offer the quick fix to healthy church life and serious church growth. But holiness has never, ever, not once been an explicitly marked feature of any church ministry I have known. Holiness is the most important factor in the church's effectiveness and yet the most neglected factor in her daily life. Jonathan Edwards said,

> A true sign of a work of God is a delight in the excellency of God—his holy character and his work.[10]

Where God's holiness is delighted in, God is at work; where holiness is neglected, God is replaced. The distinguished Bible teacher Dr. Martyn Lloyd-Jones said that the priority for the church must be the reviving of believers, a pursuing of the Spirit for the church with the result that

> they are humbled, they are convicted of sin, they are terrified at themselves. Many of them feel that they have never been Christians. And they come to see the great salvation of God in all its glory and to feel its power.[11]

The fruits are powerful praying and powerful preaching, which have an impact on society—mass conversions, expanding churches, new causes led by the Spirit, and many people offering themselves for ministry.

The great theme of Evan Roberts, who led the Welsh Revival, was holiness. Each night in the early part of the revival, he repeated this message that exhorted the church to consecrate herself to God:

- Confess before God every sin in our past life that has not been confessed.
- Remove everything that is doubtful in our lives.
- Total surrender: Say and do all that the Spirit tells us.
- Make a public confession of Christ.[12]

Those four simple points, addressing themselves to God's holiness, man's sinfulness, and consecration to God's will, stirred a compromised and complacent church to get consecrated to God. And when she did, God came; he transformed Wales and in fact the worldwide church, as the Welsh revival flame jumped to North America, China, India, Korea, and Africa.

All true revivals have been revivals of holiness, where love for God's perfections and hatred of man's imperfections are prominent themes. When God moves on a community, confession of sin becomes central. In fact, revival often begins with such a sense of God's holiness that men and women cry aloud, even fainting with intense emotion, due to their agonies over the sins exposed by God's searching purity. When the church gets serious about holiness and sick with sinfulness, then and only then may we expect God to get serious with us. If we would see God do extraordinary things in our society, we need to get to that place—we need to learn to cry with the Victorian Scottish saint

Robert Murray McCheyne: "Lord, make me as holy as a saved sinner can be."

A HOLY CHURCH CAN REVIVE HOLINESS IN THE WORLD

Once God's people are consecrated, the Lord does amazing things among them—socially transforming things. There is an undeniable link between a consecrated church, a visitation of God, and a transformation of society. Social holiness flows from a church getting holy. Though not all get saved in revival, society does get changed. Again, Jonathan Edwards observed,

> None are converted but what are reformed … [but] some men are reformed that are not yet converted.[13]

Stuart Piggin said that, when the church is revived, there is a massive assault on the Evil One in his structures in society:

> Sin is always curbed in the community as even unbelievers see the power of goodness and holiness [manifest in the church].[14]

The Puritan revival laid a foundation for the English parliamentary democracy that later became a model for good government throughout the world. The eighteenth-century Great Awakening under Wesley and Whitefield pulled a nation back from the brink of civil war. The famous English revival of 1859 led directly to social transformation through public health reforms, sanitation and housing laws, slum clearance programs, educational reforms, provision of public libraries, museums, art galleries, reforms in hospital care, and the building of new hospitals. A revival of holiness in the church brings a moral conscience to society that results in moral change. God does amazing things among us when we consecrate ourselves.

The Welsh revival in 1904 was marked by a passion for purity. Holiness was the consistent theme as one hundred thousand new converts rejected their sinful lives, confessed Christ, and joined the church. But this change in their lives had a profound impact on culture. It was reported that pit ponies could no longer work because they didn't recognize the commands of the converted miners, who no longer swore, cursed, and beat the ponies. The standard of living went up, and health and literacy improved as money previously wasted on alcohol was invested in the home, clothing, food, and books. Pubs closed as teetotalism became the norm. Magistrates were left with fewer cases to try as crime diminished. Old debts were paid. The streets were peaceful; swearing was seldom heard. Cardiff Jail had a period with no inmates. New Year's Eve week, there was not one arrest for drunkenness. The police were employed to do nothing.

One account of the Welsh revival detailed the work of a minister called Principal Edwards, who

> seems to revel in rescue work; it is the joy of his life. All sorts of conditions of men and women, drunkards, gamblers, debauchers, prostitutes, prodigals, have been coming in night after night where they

have found salvation.... Over 600 have been converted, many of whom saved from the lowest depths of sin.[15]

What would your town or city look like if the most notorious six hundred sinners were saved and sanctified? Can you imagine that? That is revival!

During a revival led by the evangelist Billy Sunday in Wilkes Barnes, Pennsylvania, in the early twentieth century, cab drivers were furious because their takings were down, due in no small part to fewer customers needing lifts to the red-light district. Brothels closed down and moved out of town. Following the 1959 Billy Graham crusade to Australia, there was an unprecedented reversal in the crime rate, a decline in the rate of illegitimate births, and reduced liquor consumption.[16] During the Brownsville revival in Florida in the 1990s, police would sometimes offer criminals a choice—to the cell or to the revival?

So, here then is God's economy: personal holiness, leading to church holiness, leading to national holiness. Who of us will be first to say, "Lord, start with me"?

GOD'S PRINCIPLE OF SOCIAL TRANSFORMATION

How do I consecrate myself in order that I might see God do amazing things in the church and, through the church, in society? I believe 2 Chronicles 7:14 offers a divine principle and a promise, as inviolable as a law of nature. This is God's word to Solomon at the dedication of the temple. Though initially it related directly to Israel in their covenant relationship with God, it reveals the *modus operandi* of the unchanging God, his will and his ways. As Paul said, these things were written for our learning (Rom. 15:4). God doesn't leave us guessing—he instructs us himself:

> *If my people, who are called by my name, will humble themselves and pray and seek my face and turn from their wicked ways, then will I hear from heaven and will forgive their sin and will heal their land.*

- *If*—the choice is ours.
- *my people*—don't expect sinners to start a revival; God's people must go first.
- *called by my name*—let us live up to our name: saints, Christians, little Christs.
- *humble themselves*—the hardest thing … get out of the way and put God first.
- *and pray*—we must open full, frank, and faithful communication with God.
- *and seek my face*—not just God's hand for handouts, but his face; intimacy.
- *and turn from their wicked ways*—turn away, reject, renounce, remove all sin.
- *then*—not before these conditions are met can we expect the promise fulfilled.
- *will I*—God's promise is emphatic.
- *hear from heaven*—God will always be attentive to the repentant.

- *and will forgive their sin*—God will remove the stain of sin and penalty of sin.
- *and will heal their land*—sin damages lives and lands: Once sin is forgiven, God can transform a land.

So there we have it—God will do amazing things among us if we consecrate ourselves, if we set ourselves apart for him as holy. We have studied in depth what a holy life looks like and how we may move toward that. All that is left is one question, both for you, the reader, and for me, the writer:

Will I go for it?

Bibliography

These are the publications quoted in the main text, listed in alphabetical order of author's or editor's surname. Page and volume references are given in the endnotes.

Adams, Kevin. *A Diary of Revival*. Farnham, Surrey, UK: Crusade for World Revival, 2004.

Barrett, C. K. *The Gospel According to St. John*. London: Society for Promoting Christian Knowledge, 1978.

Barth, Karl. *Church Dogmatics*. London: Continuum, T&T Clark, 1975.

———*Prayer*. Louisville, KY: Westminster John Knox Press, 1952.

Barton, Stephen, ed. *Holiness: Past and Present*. London: Continuum, T&T Clark, 2003.

Bassett, Paul, ed. *Great Holiness Classics*. Vol. 1, *Holiness Teaching*. Kansas City, MO: Beacon Hill Press, 1997.

Bauer, Walter, and Frederick Danker. *A Greek-English Lexicon of the New Testament*. Edited by William Arndt, F. Wilbur Gingrich, and Frederick Danker. Chicago: University of Chicago Press, 1979.

Baxter, J. Sidlow. *A New Call to Holiness*. Grand Rapids, MI: Kregel, 1993.

———*Explore the Book*. Grand Rapids, MI: Zondervan, 1987.

———*His Deeper Work in Us*. Grand Rapids, MI: Kregel, 1993.

Berkhof, Hendrikus. *The Christian Faith*. Grand Rapids, MI: Eerdmans, 1990.

Berkhof, Louis. *Systematic Theology*. Grand Rapids, MI: Eerdmans/Banner of Truth, 1971.

Berkouwer, G. C. *Studies in Dogmatics: Faith and Sanctification*. Grand Rapids, MI: Eerdmans, 1952.

Blackaby, Henry. *Holiness*. Nashville, TN: Thomas Nelson, 2003.

Bonhoeffer, Dietrich. *The Cost of Discipleship*. New York: Touchstone, 1995.

Bounds, E. M. *Power Through Prayer*. New Kensington, PA: Whitaker House, 1983.

———*Purpose in Prayer*. Grand Rapids, MI: Fleming H. Revell, 1920.

Breidlid, Anders, Frederick Brogger, Oyvind Gulliksen, and Torbjorn Sirevag, eds. *American Culture*. New York: Routledge, 1995.

Bridges, Jerry. *The Pursuit of Holiness*. Colorado Springs, CO: NavPress, 1978.

Brower, Kent. *Holiness in the Gospels*. Kansas City, MO: Beacon Hill Press, 2005.

Brower, Kent, and Andy Johnson, eds. *Holiness and Ecclesiology in the New Testament*. Grand Rapids, MI: Eerdmans, 2007.

Brown, Colin, ed. *New International Dictionary of New Testament Theology*. Grand Rapids, MI: Zondervan, 1986.

Bruce, F. F. *The Epistle to the Galatians*. Grand Rapids, MI: Eerdmans, 1982.

Calvin, John. *Institutes of the Christian Religion*. Translated by Ford Lewis Battles. Edited by John McNeill. Louisville, KY: Westminster John Knox Press, 1960.

Carey, George. *I Believe in Man*. London: Hodder & Stoughton, 1977.

Cranfield, C. E. B. *The Epistle to the Romans*. London: Continuum, T&T Clark, 1975, 1979.

Davies, W. D., and D. C. Allison. *Matthew*. London: Continuum, T&T Clark, 1997.

Edwards, Brian. *Revival*. Darlington, UK: Evangelical Press, 1990.

Edwards, Gene. *The Secret of the Christian Life*. Jacksonville, FL: Seedsowers, 2000.

Edwards, Jonathan. *The Diary and Journal of David Brainerd*. Edinburgh: Banner of Truth, 2007.

———*Religious Affections*. Edited by John Smith. New Haven, CT: Yale University Press, 1959.

Eliot, T. S. "Little Gidding." *Four Quartets*. Orlando, FL: Harcourt, 1971.

Erickson, Millard. *Christian Theology*. Grand Rapids, MI: Baker, Baker Academic, 1998.

Fee, Gordon. *God's Empowering Presence*. Peabody, MA: Hendrickson, 1994.

Ferguson, Sinclair. *The Holy Spirit*. Downers Grove, IL: InterVarsity Press, 1996.

Forsyth, P. T. *Missions in State and Church: Sermons and Addresses*. London: Hodder & Stoughton, 1908.

———*The Work of Christ*. London: Hodder & Stoughton, 1910.

France, R. T. *The Gospel of Matthew*. Grand Rapids, MI: Eerdmans, 2007.

Freedman, David Noel, ed. *Anchor Bible Dictionary*. Vol. 3. New York: Doubleday, 1992.

Fung, R. Y. K. *Epistle to the Galatians*. Grand Rapids, MI: Eerdmans, 1988.

Gaybba, Brian. *The Spirit of Love*. London: Geoffrey Chapman, 1987.

Greathouse, William. *Wholeness in Christ*. Kansas City, MO: Beacon Hill Press, 1998.

Green, Joel, Scot McKnight, and I. Howard Marshall, eds. *Dictionary of Jesus and the Gospels*. Downers Grove, IL: InterVarsity Press, 1992.

Harris, Murray. *Second Epistle to the Corinthians*. Grand Rapids, MI: Eerdmans, 2005.

Hawthorne, Gerald, Ralph Martin, and Daniel Reid, eds. *Dictionary of Paul and His Letters*. Downers Grove, IL: InterVarsity Press, 1993.

Hulse, Erroll. *Give Him No Rest*. Darlington, UK: Evangelical Press, 2006.

Jeremias, Joachim. *Jerusalem in the Time of Jesus*. London: SCM Press, 1969.

Jobes, Karen. *1 Peter*. Grand Rapids, MI: Baker, 2005.

Kelly, J. N. D. *Early Christian Doctrines*. New York: HarperCollins, 1978.

Kidner, Derek. *Genesis*. London: Tyndale Press, 1967.

Köberle, Adolf. *The Quest for Holiness*. Eugene, OR: Wipf and Stock, 2004.

Lamott, Anne. *Plan B.* New York: Penguin, Riverhead, 2005.

Larsen, Scott, ed. *Indelible Ink.* Colorado Springs, CO: WaterBrook, 2003.

Lewis, C. S. *Letters to an American Lady.* Grand Rapids, MI: Eerdmans, 1971.

————*Letters to Malcolm: Chiefly on Prayer.* New York: Harcourt, Brace & World, 1964.

————*The Great Divorce.* New York: HarperCollins, 2001.

Lloyd-Jones, Martyn. *Romans.* Vol. 5, *The New Man.* Carlisle, PA: Banner of Truth, 1972.

Lowe, Karen. *Carriers of the Fire.* Llanelli, UK: Shedhead Publications, 2004.

Mantle, John Gregory. *Beyond Humiliation.* Washington, D.C.: Testimony Book Ministry, 1974.

Martin, Ralph. *The Fulfillment of All Desire.* Steubenville, OH: Emmaus Road Publishing, 2006.

McDermott, Gerald. *Seeing God.* Vancouver, BC: Regent College, 2000.

Mellor, Victoria. "Edwards and the Affections." Master's thesis, University of Bangor, 2006.

Moltmann, Jürgen. *Spirit of Life.* London: SCM Press, 1992.

Murray, Andrew. *Abide in Christ.* Radford, VA: Wilder Publications, 2008.

————*The Spirit of Christ.* Bloomington, MN: Bethany House, 1984.

Nicholl, Donald. *Holiness.* London: DLT, 2004.

Oswalt, John. *Called to Be Holy.* Nappanee, IN: Evangel, 1999.

————*The Book of Isaiah.* Grand Rapids, MI: Eerdmans, 1986.

Otto, Rudolf. *The Idea of the Holy.* Oxford: Oxford University Press, 1923.

Owen, John. *The Glory of Christ.* Carlisle, PA: Banner of Truth, 1994.

————*The Holy Spirit.* Geanies House, Fern, Scotland: Christian Focus, 2005.

Pannenberg, Wolfhart. *Systematic Theology.* Grand Rapids, MI: Eerdmans, 1998.

Peterson, David. *Possessed by God.* Downers Grove, IL: InterVarsity Press, 1995.

Piggin, Stuart. *Firestorm of the Lord.* Milton Keynes, UK: Paternoster, 2000.

Rahner, Karl, ed. *Sacramentum Mundi*. Vol. 6, s.v. "Sin." Montreal, Canada: Palm, 1970.

Ryken, Leland, James Wilhoit, and Tremper Longman III, eds. *Dictionary of Biblical Imagery*. Downers Grove, IL: InterVarsity Press, 1998.

Ryle, J. C. *Holiness*. Darlington, UK: Evangelical Press, 1979.

Ryle, J. C. *Expository Thoughts on the Gospel of John*. Carlisle, PA: Banner of Truth, 1987.

Smalley, Stephen. *1, 2, 3 John*. Nashville, TN: Thomas Nelson, 1984.

Stott, John. *Men Made New*. Grand Rapids, MI: Baker, 1988.

————*The Message of Romans*. Downers Grove, IL: InterVarsity Press, 1994.

Sproul, R. C. *The Holiness of God*. Wheaton, IL: Tyndale, 1985.

Strong, A. H. *Systematic Theology*. Valley Forge, PA: The Judson Press, 1907.

Thomas, J. C. *The Pentecostal Commentary on 1 John, 2 John, 3 John*, London: Continuum, T&T Clark, 2004.

Thrall, Margaret. *2 Corinthians*. London: Continuum, T&T Clark, 1994.

Tozer, A. W. *That Incredible Christian*. Camp Hill, PA: Christian Publications, 1986.

————*The Knowledge of the Holy*. New York: HarperOne, 1978.

Waetjen, H. C. *The Gospel of the Beloved Disciple*. London: Continuum, T&T Clark, 2001.

Webster, John. *Holiness*. Grand Rapids, MI: Eerdmans, 2003.

Wenham, Gordon. *Word Biblical Commentary*. Vol. 1, *Genesis 1–15*. Milton Keynes, UK: Word, 1991.

————*The Book of Leviticus*. Grand Rapids, MI: Eerdmans, 1978.

Williams, J. Rodman. *Renewal Theology*. Grand Rapids, MI: Zondervan, 1988.

Woudstra, M. H. *The Book of Joshua*. Grand Rapids, MI: Eerdmans, 1981.

Wright, N. T. *Colossians and Philemon*. Downers Grove, IL: InterVarsity Press, 1987.

Zacharias, Ravi. *Cries of the Heart*. Dallas: Word, 1998.

Notes

Chapter 1: The Longing to Be Holy

1. Author's paraphrase.
2. C. S. Lewis, *Letters to an American Lady*, 19.
3. John Oswalt, *Called to Be Holy*, 3.
4. "Holy," *Oxford English Dictionary*, 7: 318–19.
5. David Wright, "Holiness in the Old Testament," ed. David Noel Freedman, 237–49.
6. Walter Bauer and Frederick Danker, "Hagiazo, Hagios," 8–9.
7. Thanks to John Martin for this insight of understanding holiness through its association.
8. David Peterson, 11.
9. Discussed in Stephen Barton, 6.
10. Ibid., xvi.
11. Gene Edwards, 94.
12. Barton, xvii.
13. H. L. Mencken, *A Book of Burlesques*, "Sententiæ" (1920).
14. Anne Lamott, 66.
15. Melissa Raphael, "Holiness *in extremis:* Jewish Women's Resistance to the Profane in Auschwitz," ed. Barton, 381–401.

Chapter 2: The Holiness of God

1. P. T Forsyth, *The Work of Christ,* 126–27.
2. Ibid., 79.
3. Used with permission.
4. Quoted in William Greathouse, 18.
5. A. W. Tozer, *The Knowledge of the Holy,* 104.
6. Jerry Bridges, 22.
7. John Webster, 31.
8. Ibid., 42.
9. Bridges, 22.
10. Greathouse, 19.
11. Gerald McDermott, 109.
12. Karl Barth, *Church Dogmatics,* 2:351.
13. Hendrikus Berkhof, 130.
14. My friend Mark Davies asked this profound question of me, as well as suggested possible answers.
15. J. Sidlow Baxter, *Explore the Book,* 88.
16. John Oswalt, *The Book of Isaiah,* 176–77.
17. Could it be that Satan, a fallen angel of light, was once a seraph who appeared as a serpent to Adam and Eve?
18. Oswalt, *The Book of Isaiah,* 181.
19. R. Moberly, "Holy, Holy, Holy—Isaiah's Vision of God," ed. Stephen Barton, 126.
20. Oswalt, *The Book of Isaiah,* 181.
21. Ibid., 184.
22. Ibid., 180.
23. Eliot, 57. (Used to great effect to conclude Moberly's fine treatment of this theme and shamelessly pinched by me.)

Chapter 3: The Sinfulness of Us

1. Quoted in Jonathan Edwards, *The Diary and Journal of David Brainerd.*
2. J. C. Ryle, *Holiness,* 4.
3. C. S. Lewis, *Letters to Malcolm: Chiefly on Prayer,* 127.

4. Karl Rahner, 87.

5. Wolfhart Pannenberg, 2:233, 237.

6. See George Carey.

7. *The New Shorter Oxford English Dictionary,* s.v. "Sin."

8. W. Günther, "Sin," ed. Colin Brown, 3:578.

9. Ibid.

10. Rahner, 87.

11. Pannenberg, 239.

12. Günther, ed. Brown, 573–578.

13. Ibid., 579.

14. Ryle, *Holiness,* 2.

15. Ibid., 4.

16. Ibid.

17. Gordon Wenham, *Word Biblical Commentary,* vol. 1, *Genesis 1–15,* 73.

18. Derek Kidner, 70.

19. See Leland Ryken, James Wilhoit, and Tremper Longman III, eds., s.v. "Temple," 849.

20. Interview with Joan Collins, *The Sunday Express.* I wrote this quote down many years ago and no longer have access to the original source or date of publication.

21. Malcolm Muggeridge, quoted in Ravi Zacharias, 111.

Chapter 4: The Beckoning of the Holy

1. R. C. Sproul, 158.

2. George Herbert, "Love Bade Me Welcome," ed. Arthur Quiller-Couch, *The Oxford Book of English Verse: 1250–1900* (Oxford: Clarendon, 1919).

3. Karl Barth, *Church Dogmatics,* 2:364.

4. Gordon Wenham, *The Book of Leviticus,* 180.

5. Karen Jobes, 113.

6. Jerry Bridges, 21.

7. Barth, *Church Dogmatics,* 2:358.

8. J. N. D. Kelly, 357.

9. Ibid.

10. Ibid., 360.

11. Ibid.

12. Augustine of Hippo, "On Man's Perfection in Righteousness," http://www.newadvent.org/fathers/1504.htm.

13. John Wesley, *A Plain Account of Christian Perfection*, 11:366–446. These are Wesley's reflections between 1725 and 1777. See also http://gbgm-umc.org/Umhistory/Wesley/perfect1.html.

14. Ibid.

15. Ibid., 109.

16. Paul Bassett, 38.

17. Ibid.

18. J. Rodman Williams, 270.

19. Donald Hagner, "Holiness and Ecclesiology: The Church in Matthew," ed. Kent Brower and Andy Johnson, 55.

20. Ralph Martin, 1.

21. Ibid., 4–5.

22. Ibid., 5.

23. Dietrich Bonhoeffer, 153.

24. A. W. Tozer, *That Incredible Christian*, 40.

25. Joe Darion, "The Impossible Dream (The Quest)," *Man of La Mancha* © 1965 Andrew Scott Inc., Helena Music Corp., Sam Fox Publ. Co. Inc.

Chapter 5: Unholy Religion

1. Gerard Hughes, quoted in Donald Nicholl.

2. Ralph Martin, 2.

3. C. S. Lewis, *Letters to an American Lady*, 40.

4. Dietrich Müller, "Pharisee," ed. Colin Brown, 2:810.

5. Kent Brower and Andy Johnson, eds., 30.

6. I am drawing heavily in this section on the detailed study by Joachim Jeremias, 247–53.

7. See also James Dunn, "Jesus and Holiness—the Challenge to Purity," ed. Barton, 174.

8. Ibid., 175.

9. Brower and Johnson, 30.

10. Rabbi Shammai, quoted in Müller, "Pharisee," ed. Brown, 2:811.

11. Brower and Johnson, 30–32.

12. S. Westerholm, "Pharisees," ed. Joel Green, Scot McKnight, I. Howard Marshall, 612.

13. Müller, "Pharisee," ed. Brown, 2:813.

14. W. D. Davies and D. C. Allison, 3:307.

15. R. T. France, 855.

16. Müller, "Pharisee," ed. Brown, 2:812.

17. I am indebted to and relying on the perceptive insights of John Oswalt's *Called to Be Holy,* 185–95.

18. Ibid., 187.

19. Ibid., 195.

Chapter 6: Without Blame

1. John Stott, *Men Made New,* 81.

2. William Shakespeare, *Macbeth,* ed. Horace Howard Furness (Philadelphia: J. B. Lippincott Company, 1873), 5.1.33–34. References are to act, scene, and line.

3. Augustus Toplady, "Rock of Ages," public domain.

4. J. Rodman Williams, 2:64.

5. Adolf Köberle, 58.

6. John Calvin, 651.

7. Köberle, 58.

8. Martin Luther, quoted in a sermon by C. H. Spurgeon, at the Metropolitan Tabernacle, Newington, March 6, 1890.

Chapter 7: Without Fault

1. J. C. Ryle, "Holiness," sermon, http://clydemartin.com/holiness.html.

2. Jonathan Edwards, 366.

3. S. E. Porter, "Holiness/Sanctification," ed. Gerald Hawthorne, Ralph Martin, and Daniel Reid, 398.

4. I am drawing in part on a list given by J. C. Ryle, *Holiness,* 37–39.

5. John Owen, *The Holy Spirit*, 308.

6. Jonathan Edwards, quoted in Victoria Mellor.

7. A. H. Strong, 869.

8. Louis Berkhof, 532.

9. Millard Erickson, 971.

10. Sinclair Ferguson, 139.

11. Jürgen Moltmann, 174.

12. S. E. Porter, "Holiness/Sanctification," ed. Hawthorne, Martin, and Reid, 397–98.

13. Brian Doerksen, "Refiner's Fire," © 1990 Mercy/Vineyard Publishing.

14. "2 Corinthians 7:1," *Robertson's Word Pictures of the New Testament*, http://www.biblestudytools.com/commentaries/robertsons-word-pictures/2-corinthians/2-corinthians-7-1.html.

15. Murray Harris, 513.

16. C. S. Lewis, *The Great Divorce*, 128.

17. Quoted at length in J. Sidlow Baxter, *His Deeper Work in Us*, 81.

18. Ibid.

19. See full treatment at http://www.frontlinemin.org/higherlife.asp.

20. John Stott, quoted in ed. Scott Larsen, 21.

21. See G. C. Berkouwer, 105.

22. Margaret Thrall, 480.

23. J. Sidlow Baxter, *His Deeper Work in Us*, 98.

24. Ibid., 84, 98.

25. John Stott, quoted in ed. Scott Larsen, 20.

26. J. C. Ryle, *Holiness*, 27.

27. Thomas Cranmer, "Thirty-Nine Articles: Number 15," *Book of Common Prayer*.

Chapter 8: Jesus: The Holy One of God

1. P. T. Forsyth, *Missions in State and Church: Sermons and Addresses*, 233.

2. Chick Yuill, quoted in Kent Brower, 43.

3. N. T. Wright, 83.

4. G. C. Berkouwer, 135.

5. I am drawing on the excellent summary by R. A. Torrey on the sinlessness of Christ, found at http://www.whatthebibleteaches.com/wbt_180.htm.

6. Brower, 129.

7. Ibid.

Chapter 9: Wanted: Dead and Alive

1. Karl Barth, *Prayer,* 17–18.

2. For all of the passages from Romans in this chapter I use the NASB due to its accuracy in translating verb tenses.

3. Martyn Lloyd-Jones.

4. Ibid., 29–30.

5. James Swan, "Did Luther Say 'Be a sinner and sin boldly'?", http://www.ntrmin.org/Be%20a%20sinner%20and%20sin%20boldly%20web.htm#a1 (accessed March 10, 2010).

6. Winston Churchill (speech, Harrow School, Harrow, UK, October 29, 1941).

7. See full treatment in C. E. B. Cranfield, 299–300.

8. Ibid., 299.

9. William Sanday and Arthur Headlam, quoted in Cranfield, 298.

10. Charles Wesley, "O For a Thousand Tongues to Sing," 1738, public domain.

11. Cranfield, 317.

12. William Greathouse, 101.

13. John Stott, *The Message of Romans,* 176.

14. John Gregory Mantle.

Chapter 10: Holy Spirit, Holy Living

1. Gordon Fee, 137.

2. I have written at length on sanctification and the Spirit in my book *God Inside Out* (Eastbourne, UK: Kingsway, 2007, 154–73). Some of this chapter draws on the material there.

3. Andrew Murray, *The Spirit of Christ,* 273.

4. Jürgen Moltmann, 164.

5. John Calvin, 3.xiv.1. References are to book, section, and paragraph.

6. Ibid., 3.xiv.2.

7. *The Lutheran Formula of Concord,* Proposition II, 65–66.

8. John Owen, *The Holy Spirit,* 308.

9. Ibid.

10. Ibid., 240–350, esp. 307–11.

11. See full treatment by Roderick Macleod at http://www.fpchurch.org.uk.

12. Jonathan Edwards, quoted in Victoria Mellor.

13. Brian Gaybba, 213–16.

14. John Wesley, quoted in J. Sidlow Baxter, *His Deeper Work in Us,* 192.

15. Ibid.

16. J. Sidlow Baxter, *A New Call to Holiness,* 171.

17. Louis Berkhof, 532.

18. Millard Erickson, 971.

19. R. Y. K. Fung, 253.

20. Ibid., 249.

21. F. F. Bruce, 219.

Chapter 11: Staying Holy

1. Stephen Smalley, 158.

2. J. C. Thomas, 157.

3. Walter Bauer and Frederick Danker, s.v. "Meno," 503.

4. H. C. Waetjen, 327.

5. C. K. Barrett, 473.

6. J. C.Ryle, *Expository Thoughts on the Gospel of John,* note on 15:1–6

7. Andrew Murray, *Abide in Christ.*

8. Charles Finney, "Abiding in Christ and Not Sinning," *Oberlin Evangelist,* December 22, 1818.

9. Waetjen, 349.

10. E. M. Bounds, *Purpose in Prayer,* 48.

11. "Mr. John Bunyan's Dying Sayings," *Bunyan's Works,* ed. George Offor (1861), http://acacia.pair.com/Acacia.John.Bunyan/Sermons.Allegories/Bunyan.Dying.Sayings/4.html.

12. C. S. Lewis, *Letters to Malcolm: Chiefly on Prayer,* 92.

13. John Owen, *The Glory of Christ,* 115.

Chapter 12: When Holiness Spreads Like Fire

1. M. H. Woudstra, 81.

2. Jim Wallis (speech, the National Presbyterian Evangelism Conference, Nashville, Tennessee, August 31, 2007).

3. J. Edwin Orr, quoted in Erroll Hulse, 19.

4. Jonathan Edwards, quoted in eds. Anders Breidlid, Frederick Brogger, Oyvind Gulliksen, and Torbjorn Sirevag, 237.

5. Henry Blackaby, 72.

6. Brian Edwards, 60.

7. E. M. Bounds, *Power Through Prayer.*

8. There is a famous quote spoken to D. L. Moody by Henry Vardey that inspired Moody in his evangelistic zeal: "The world has yet to see what God can do through one man fully devoted to him."

9. Brian Edwards, 59.

10. Jonathan Edwards, quoted in Hulse, 24.

11. Martyn Lloyd-Jones, quoted in Hulse, 18.

12. Kevin Adams, 94.

13. Jonathan Edwards, quoted in Stuart Piggin, 23.

14. Piggin, 22–23.

15. Karen Lowe.

16. Piggin, 23.

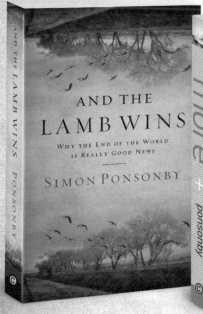